My Brother, t

WITHDRAWN

Georg Ratzinger

My Brother, the Pope

As told to
Michael Hesemann

Translated by Michael J. Miller

IGNATIUS PRESS   SAN FRANCISCO

Original German edition:

Mein Bruder, der Papst

© 2011 by F. A. Herbig Verlag, Munich

Cover photograph:
With the *Domspatzen* in the Sistine Chapel:
Pope Benedict XVI thanks his brother, Msgr. Georg Ratzinger
© *L'Osservatore Romano*

Cover design by Roxanne Mei Lum

© 2011 by Ignatius Press, San Francisco
All rights reserved
ISBN 978-1-58617-704-1
Library of Congress Control Number 2011940712
Printed in the United States of America ∞

From the beginning of my life, my brother has always been for me not only a companion, but also a trustworthy guide. For me he has been a point of orientation and of reference with the clarity and determination of his decisions. He has always shown me the path to take, even in difficult situations. . . . My brother has pointed out that since then, we have arrived at the last stage of our lives, at old age. The days left to live progressively diminish. But also in this stage my brother helps me to accept with serenity, with humility, and with courage the weight of each day.

Pope Benedict XVI
August 21, 2008[1]

---

[1] On the occasion of the conferral of the honorary citizenship of Castel Gandolfo on his brother, Monsignor Georg Ratzinger.

Contents

Introduction

by Michael Hesemann

The idea for this book was born in an extremely unusual place, namely, in the shrine in Absam, not far from Innsbruck in Tyrol. In it pilgrims venerate an image of Mary that is quite different from the Black Madonna of Czestochowa in Poland, the "Comforter of the Afflicted" in Kevelaer in the Rhineland, or any other miraculous image of the Mother of God in one of the many places of pilgrimage in old Europe. For it is the only one in the Old World that claims to be "not made by human hands" and is thus comparable only to the tilma in Guadalupe, Mexico. How it came to be is in any case a riddle that science to this day cannot answer. On January 17, 1797, the farm girl Rosina Bucher was sitting with her needlework at a window of the room on the ground floor of her parents' house, through which the setting sun was shining. At that moment, as she declared later for the official record, a young woman looked at her through the windowpane, and her face never disappeared from it again. From then on, it was literally branded into the glass like a rough drawing, the head leaning gently to one side, the mouth closed, a kerchief tied around her head. Her serious expression, which is both sad and hopeful, touches the viewer's heart deeply. It is as though she were looking in at our world once again through the window of our heavenly Father's house.

Now 1797 was a difficult year for the Church. The cool, sometimes ice-cold wind of the Enlightenment had long since wafted through the last mountain village in Tyrol, Napoleon's troops were implementing the values of the French Revolution, with military force if needed, and they were even marching against Rome and the pope. So the miraculous image of Absam, too, met at first with skepticism and rejection. Since it was thought to be a painting on glass, the pane was immediately scrubbed thoroughly several times, whereupon the Marian image vanished, only to reappear again on the dry pane in its former splendor. Even attempts to sand it off or to remove it permanently with acid failed miserably. Thus the diocesan chancery relented after the investigations were completed and allowed the windowpane with the image to be transferred to Saint Michael's Church in Absam. It is still there today, set in a splendid golden reliquary and venerated by large numbers of pilgrims.

Our Lady of Absam answered prayers very effectively, as a whole warehouse of thank-you gifts from pilgrims testifies (usually *ex voto* plaques). But many also liked to be married in Absam; couples from all parts of Tyrol wanted to tie the matrimonial knot in the presence of the Mother of God who had appeared so miraculously. This was true also of a couple from Mühlbach near Oberaudorf in Bavaria who were wed in Absam on July 13, 1885: Maria Tauber-Peintner (1855–1930) and the baker Isidor Rieger (1860–1912). "The bride is well instructed in religion", the pastor noted in the record after interviewing her—unusually well for a simple maidservant. Thirty-five years later, her daughter Maria would stand at the altar for her wedding, and this time the Mother of God had arranged the marriage personally, so to speak. At any rate, the daughter Maria had met her husband through an advertisement placed in the *Altöttinger Liebfrauenboten*, the in-house publication of Altötting, the most important Marian shrine and place of pilgrimage in all Bavaria. The notice read as follows:

> Mid-level government official, single, Catholic, 43 years old, with an irreproachable record, from the country, seeks to marry in the near future a good Catholic girl who is tidy and a good cook and

can do all the household chores and is also proficient at sewing and has her own furnishings.

This was already the second attempt by the policeman Joseph Ratzinger to find a wife at last; the first, made in March 1920, evidently met with no success. The second notice appeared in July 1920, and Maria Peintner answered it.[1] It must have been love at first sight. At any rate, the couple married just four months later, on November 9, 1920, in Pleiskirchen in the district of Altötting. Thirteen months later, on December 7, 1921, their first child came into the world, a girl, who naturally was baptized with the name Maria. The first son, born likewise in Pleiskirchen on January 15, 1924, was to be named Georg. His younger brother, who first saw the light of day on April 16, 1927, in Marktl (Altötting), was named Joseph, after his father. Exactly 120 years after the wedding of his grandparents in Absam, on April 19, 2005, the cardinals of the Catholic Church elected the latter Joseph Ratzinger to be the 265th successor of the Apostle Peter. From then on, he would be called Benedict XVI.

The Pope from Bavaria had just celebrated the fifth anniversary of his pontificate and had made a pilgrimage to the Shroud of Jesus in Turin; as I traveled back to Germany, I took the opportunity to make a side-trip to Absam. There, at the place where it all began, I hoped to get to the bottom of the secret of the first German on the Throne of Peter since Adrian VI (1522–1523).[2] Ever since 2005, right after his election, when I had

[1] Quotation from the marriage certificate from the year 1920: "The municipal authorities of Rimsting hereby certify, for the purpose of her intended marriage, that Maria Peintner, a cook, was born on January 8, 1884, the legitimate daughter of the baker Isidore and his wife Maria Rieger, née Peintner, and is resident in the undersigned municipality. She has no children. Maria Rieger goes by the name Peintner, because to this day no official acknowledgment of paternity has been forthcoming and the necessary proofs from Tyrol cannot be recovered on account of the Italian occupation. Municipality of Rimsting, October 3, 1920—the Mayor."

[2] Adrian VI was from Utrecht, which at that time was part of the Holy Roman Empire of the German Nation. The last pope from the territory of the present-day Federal Republic of Germany was Victor II (1055–1057), the former Bishop of Eichstätt, from the line of the Counts of Dollnstein-Hirschberg.

written the biographical portrait *Benedetto!* with Yuliya Tkachova for those who would attend World Youth Day in Cologne,
I had been fascinated by his path through life and by the question of whether something like a predestination could be dis-
cerned in it. As the years went by, I increasingly wished that I
could someday have a chance to interview at length his closest
and dearest confidant since childhood, his brother, Georg.

Georg Ratzinger, who today is eighty-seven years old, lives in
Regensburg and is nothing less than a "living legend" in that
cathedral city. After all, as cathedral choirmaster, he was the one
who helped the Regensburger Domspatzen, the boys choir of
the bishop's church in Regensburg, achieve its greatest successes.
So it was by no means uncommon before the momentous year
2005 for Joseph Cardinal Ratzinger to introduce himself as "the
little brother of the famous choral director". Since the conclave,
however, Monsignor Georg Ratzinger, whom Pope John Paul II
had already appointed an "Apostolic Protonotary", is known primarily as "the brother of the Pope", despite his own impressive
accomplishments.

In December 2010, Roswitha Biersack, director of the Bavarian section of the association of papal loyalists Deutschland pro
Papa,[3] introduced me in Regensburg to the cathedral choirmaster emeritus, who at that time was still eighty-six years old. In
our conversation, it became evident that he was not opposed to
the idea of a longer interview that could be the basis of a little
book; first, however, he wanted to put impending knee surgery
behind him. He came through the operation well, and, after
completing the subsequent "rehab", he welcomed us on May 8,
2011, to the first of five sessions (which ran to as much as two
hours) in his house on Luzengasse in Regensburg. I started the
conversation by saying, "I am now your Peter Seewald", allud-
ing to his brother's interview with the journalist from Munich

---

[3] For more about the activities of the association, visit www.deutschland-pro-papa.de.

that resulted in the wonderful volume *Light of the World*. I could not have hoped for a better moment. The readings in church on that Third Sunday of Easter recalled the first sermon of Peter on the feast of Pentecost in Jerusalem. One week earlier, I had had the privilege of attending in Rome, together with one and a half million people, the beatification by Benedict XVI of his "beloved predecessor" John Paul II. The previous day, on May 7, Deutschland pro Papa had invited me to speak at a rally on the Odeonsplatz in Munich. Catholic Germany was looking forward with tremendous excitement to the papal visit in September, while the Ratzinger brothers were preparing for their joint celebration of the diamond jubilee of their priesthood: on June 29, 1951, sixty years earlier, the present pope and his brother had dedicated themselves irrevocably to the service of the Lord by their solemn declaration, "Adsum" (I am ready). This common jubilee, I think, is the best reason to look back at two priestly lives that have been so blessed.

A word on the form of this book: since these are Msgr. Georg Ratzinger's memoirs, I have dispensed with a rigid "question-and-answer" format for the sake of readability. The words of "Herr Domkapellmeister" (Mr. Choirmaster), as he prefers to be called,[4] at least in Regensburg, which have been edited stylistically and supplemented with further details, are printed in regular type, whereas my transitions, questions, interpolated remarks, and additions are *in italics*.

Naturally this book intends in the first place to secure an important source for the life history of our German pope. The testimony of his brother supplements in particular his personal memoirs, which he published while still a cardinal in 1997–1998 under the title *Milestones*. They ended rather early on, specifically with his move to Rome in 1982. The impressive career of

---

[4] According to protocol, the correct form of address after he was named Apostolic Protonotary by Pope John Paul II in 1994 is, of course, "Hochwürdigster Herr Prälat" (Most Reverend Prelate), or, in Italian, "Monsignore"!

the cathedral choirmaster Georg Ratzinger, on the other hand, plays a rather secondary role in the present work; it has already been depicted at length in Anton Zuber's excellent and very readable biography, *Der Bruder des Papstes: Georg Ratzinger und die Regensburger Domspatzen* (Freiburg, 2007).

That being said, I would like to return to my original question of whether behind this unique "German career" of a policeman's son who became the head of 1.3 billion Catholics there was more than mere chance. It is quite certain that Joseph Ratzinger never aspired to the papacy and that this, his most important mission, like so much in his life, literally fell into his lap. He himself, citing the Third Letter of John (verse 8), inscribed *Cooperatores veritatis*, "Co-workers of the truth", on his coat of arms. Yet the more I learned about his life, the more clearly it reminded me of the motto of the recently [1998] founded Emmanuel School of Mission in Altötting, where I had the privilege of holding a seminar in January 2011: "Give All—Get More!" In his life, Joseph Ratzinger, too, has always given everything so as to receive unintentionally so much more from the Lord in return. So this book might encourage young men in particular who are toying with the idea of setting out on the path to the priesthood and following their vocation despite all the interior and external obstacles. It is a path rich in blessings that gives much more in return precisely to those who expect nothing and give their all.

I was particularly impressed also, however, by Georg Ratzinger's depiction of the early, formative years of our pope. He draws the picture of a family that grew so strong through the practice of its deep faith that it could withstand all the storms of that time, even those of the godless Nazi regime. This family can serve as an example to us especially who live in a time in which more and more marriages are failing and families are being torn apart. In the United States, I heard over and over again a saying that has so much truth in it: "A family that prays together stays together!" Only the reconciling power of faith, which bestows the gift of love, makes it possible to overcome the crises in everyday family life and to communicate to children the security and the values that open for them the door to a good future.

May this book help more families to discover again for themselves the power and joy of the Christian faith and to devote themselves to prayer in common and the celebration of the Church's feast days with their children. The family is the future of the Church. Or, to put it in the Pope's words, which became the motto of his visit to Germany in September 2011: "Where God is, there is the future."

His life thus far shows how true that is.

Rome, June 29, 2011

I
Roots

We three children were all born in the vicinity of Altöt-ting, the famous place of pilgrimage dedicated to the Mother of God, but not in the same village. My sister Maria (*born December 7, 1921*) and I (*born January 15, 1924*) came into the world in Pleiskirchen; my brother, Joseph, the Holy Father (*born April 16, 1927*), was born in Marktl am Inn. Because our father was a policeman by profession, he was often transferred, as was customary at the time. In any case, several times our whole family went on pilgrimage to Altötting. The shrine there, that wonderful little church, has a long and distinguished history that goes back to the Carolingian period. Yet we did not travel there as pilgrims on account of that historical character but, rather, because we knew it is a profoundly spiritual place. Our father even belonged to the Men's Marian Congregation, a sodality that has its headquarters in Altötting and was entirely commit-ted to honoring the Mother of God. That was one reason that drew him and us to that place again and again. These pilgrim-ages to the famous Black Madonna are among our most beau-tiful childhood memories. The spiritualized atmosphere, the result of constant prayer, charmed my brother and me so that even then we were profoundly under its influence. Therefore, grow-ing up near Altötting played an important role in our lives and also in our esteem for the Mother of God. We could always entrust our cares and worries to our Lady; however small they may have been in our childhood, we always felt protected by her.

No one ever really spoke about the time before our parents' marriage. So I did not know that my grandparents had been married at another Marian shrine, in Absam. But it is nice to know that plainly the blessing of the Mother of God was upon their marriage, too.

My mother's family was originally from Tyrol. Her parents were bakers. The father, a Bavarian Swabian by the name of Isidor Rieger, was born (*on March 22, 1860*) in Welden, which is said to be a very charming place. Her grandparents had owned a mill near Brixen in South Tyrol (*which at that time was still under Austrian rule*) that was then swept away by flooding of the Rienz River. After that, the whole family emigrated to Bavaria. For the rest of her life, my grandmother yearned for her homeland. When she became sick and was gradually approaching death, she always used to say, "If only I had a bit of water from home, I would become well again." She was convinced that the water in Tyrol was quite different from Bavarian water. She also thought that "a little hatful of hay from Tyrol" was more valuable as fodder for the cattle than a whole cartful of Bavarian hay. She was just a great Tyrolean patriot.[1]

My mother, Maria Ratzinger, née Peintner, was born on January 8, 1884, in Mühlbach bei Oberaudorf (in the Rosenheim district) in the extreme southeastern part of Bavaria, and the church where she was baptized is also there. This is the same Mühlbach where the famous soccer player Bastian Schweinsteiger grew up, too. She then went to elementary school in Rimsting on Lake Chiemsee, "the Bavarian Sea". Her parents, as I said, were bakers, and so the children had to deliver the bread every morning before school. After all, the customers wanted to have their fresh rolls and breakfast bread brought right to the house. For seven years she attended the school, and then she

---

[1] Maybe that is why she insisted on being married in Absam/Tyrol, although at that point in time she had long since been living in the Bavarian town of Mühldorf.

Maria Peintner, the mother of Joseph and Georg Ratzinger, as a young woman

took various jobs as a maid. Her first employer was a first violinist in Salzburg. Zinke was his name; he was Czech and always practiced diligently. Thus she came into contact with music. Unfortunately the first violinist was very poorly paid; he always had to play additional concerts so as to be able to survive somehow, and my mother's wages were accordingly meager. Later she worked in Kufstein in a bakery. Then she found a position in Hessen with a General Zech, who lived in Hanau, and finally she went to the Hotel Neuwittelsbach in Munich, where they were looking for a cook to make puddings, which was her specialty. And so she had already seen and experienced a few things when she met my father. During our childhood, her warmth and cordiality time and again compensated for our father's strictness. She was always cheerful and friendly toward everyone and used to sing Marian hymns while washing the dishes. Above all, however, she was also a very practical, splendid wife who was never at a loss, a real Jill-of-all-trades: she was a tailor and could make soap and knew how to prepare a tasty meal from the simplest ingredients. She was particularly adept, as I mentioned, at making delicious puddings, which are still among the favorite foods of my brother and me. Her Bavarian dumplings, which had a thick crust underneath, were marvelous. They were served with vanilla sauce. We also loved her apple strudel. Good housewives know that in a real apple strudel, the dough is so thin that it is almost transparent. It is rather wide; it is pulled apart at the corners, and then the other ingredients are added, the apple filling, raisins, and all sorts of other good things. An apple strudel like that, with a paper-thin crust, is just wonderful. Then I should mention her pancakes, which she always served with *ribisl*, as she used to call currants; this was an old Tyrolean name that hardly anyone in Bavaria could make sense of. And finally, of course, I must not forget her *kaiserschmarrn*, which was simply excellent.[2]

Otherwise we lived rather simply. We grew up to be very thrifty, for on the income of an ordinary policeman we could not afford to be extravagant. Father had to manage the money carefully so that there would be enough. Still, our parents thought it was very important for us to make a proper impression. Mother, fortunately, eased the strain on the family budget considerably. First, because we always had a garden in which she grew vegetables. During the summer months we did not need to buy vegetables, because she planted and harvested lettuce, cabbage, and carrots herself. Working in the garden was her passion. Naturally, she also planted a few beautiful flowers, which gave her so much joy.

Then, too, our mother always used to knit diligently. She herself made the caps, sweaters, socks, scarves, gloves, and everything else we wore in the winter. So she just had to buy the yarn, which greatly eased the strain on our father's budget. At that

---

[2] A caramelized pancake with bits of fruit and nuts, cut into pieces, and served with fruit sauce and powdered sugar.—TRANS.

The extended Ratzinger family on the eightieth birthday of the paternal grand-mother, Katharina Ratzinger, at the Ratzinger farm in Rickering. Sitting on the ground to the left is Georg (7), to the right, Joseph (4); Maria (9) is standing in a light-colored dress; standing, on the far right, are the parents Joseph and Maria Ratzinger. Standing on the left is Uncle Anton, and sitting in front of him is their priest uncle, the Reverend Alois Ratzinger.

time, in rural areas at least, it was not customary to buy knit woolen clothing. At any rate, we always had two pairs of gloves to choose from: mittens, which left only the thumbs free, and then five-fingered gloves. For my father and for us, Mother was simply a great windfall.

I was acquainted with both my grandmothers. My mother's mother, Maria Rieger-Peintner, did not pass away until 1930. Until then she lived in Rimsting. I visited her once with my mother. She was a rather sour woman and an expert scold, so I was told.

The only thing I recall now about my grandmother on my father's side (*Katharina Ratzinger, née Schmid, 1851–1937*) is that she was a very old lady with a black kerchief. Other than that,

I unfortunately have no memories of her. I saw her only once, when she celebrated her eightieth birthday (*in 1931*). On that occasion, there was a big party with all her relatives. It was celebrated a short distance upstream along the Danube, in Altenmarkt, I think. There is even a photo of the event, which the local historian and former senior civil servant Johann Nußbaum from Rimsting published in his book about the roots of our family.[3] The original is in the possession of my relatives, the family of Anton Messerer in Rickering bei Schwanenkirchen, the place where my father was born, too. Their grandfather was one of my father's brothers.

My father's uncle was also originally from Rickering; this was my great-uncle, Doctor Georg Ratzinger, a priest and a politician who was eventually elected to the German Imperial Parliament. Our father often spoke about him and about his main published work, *Geschichte der kirchlichen Armenpflege* (A history of the Church's work for the poor), which was also his dissertation. He had written it at the suggestion of the renowned Church historian Ignaz von Döllinger. In it he demonstrated how the care for the poor that flourished during the Middle Ages ended with the Reformation. He did write other books, too, though, for example, *Die Volkswirtschaft in ihren sittlichen Grundlagen* (The moral foundations of the political economy), which was an attempt to reconnect economic theory with a Christian ethic, centered on "the social question". Moreover, he deserves credit for having been an enlightened opponent of child labor. Currently a historian from Trier, Doctor Karl-Heinz Gorges, is working on a monograph about him, and then of course I should mention Doctor Tobias Appl from Regensburg, another historian who is an assistant professor of Bavarian history and has published articles about him. He gave a talk at a conference on the

---

[3] Nußbaum, Johann, *"Poetisch und herzensgut": Die Spuren des Papstes und seiner Familie in Rimsting* (Rimsting, 2006).

life and work of my great-uncle that was held here in Regensburg in 2008.

*Doctor Georg Ratzinger (1844–1899), as a member of the Bavarian
Patriotic Party, was a member of the House of Representatives of the
Bavarian Parliament from 1875 to 1877 and a member of the German
Imperial Parliament from 1877 to 1878. From 1893 to 1899, he was
again elected to the Bavarian Parliament, first as a member of the Bavarian Farmers' Union and, then, from 1894 on, as an independent representative. As such, he then belonged again to the Imperial Parliament
from 1898 until his death one year later.*

*Ratzinger had the reputation of being an outstanding writer with an
inclination to polemics. At the height of the* Kulturkampf *that Imperial Chancellor Bismarck conducted against Catholic Germany, his writings were confiscated and he himself was arrested for interrogation. For
a time, he was editor-in-chief of the* Fränkisches Volksblatt *in Würzburg.
He was one of the most important pioneers in German Catholic jour-
nalism. As a conservative disciple of Döllinger, he was regarded with
suspicion by the State but also by ecclesiastical circles loyal to the State,
which made an academic career as a Church historian impossible. For
that reason alone, he went into politics. He described himself as "anti-
imperial" and as a "clerical-socialist". He rejected Prussia's militaristic
striving to become a great power. In his opinion, militarism was a burden that fell chiefly on the shoulders of taxpaying workers and farmers
and served the monopolistic ambitions of high finance. He recognized
and foresaw as early as 1895 that these militaristic tendencies would
end in a world war. He was convinced that such a fate could be warded
off only by reorganizing the State according to the principles of Catholic
social teaching.*

*Even during his lifetime, Ratzinger's career was accompanied by var-
ious attempts to slander him. Today his undoubtedly considerable accom-
plishment as a Catholic social reformer is overshadowed by the accusation
that he was the author of two anti-Semitic works published under the
names "Doctor Robert Waldhausen" and "Doctor Gottfried Wolf".*

Father spoke well of him, but then we never learned anything in particular about him. It was just that we knew and were glad that among our ancestors there was a figure who had played a certain part and had achieved something of significance. In any case, his example had nothing to do with our decision to become priests. We never read his writings in my family, and his opinion about the Jews, which he allegedly did not even publish under his own name, was not something we knew about.

If we are to believe the family tree that hangs in the museum of the papal house in Marktl am Inn, the Ratzingers were an old farming family. Their genealogy can be traced uninterruptedly back to the year 1600, when one Georg Ratzinger, a farmer in Ratzing in the Diocese of Passau, was first mentioned in the church records. In fact, their roots extend much farther back. As the historian Herbert Wurster demonstrated at the above-mentioned scholarly conference about Doctor Georg Ratzinger, the family goes back to one Razi, who lived in the late tenth century in Sandbach in the Diocese of Passau. As the entry from the years 947–970 indicates, he was employed by the Church of Passau and perhaps even founded the hamlet of Ratzing, which is located 0.6 mile from Sandbach. From him was probably descended an official by the name of Dietricus de Rezinge, who appeared in the records of the monastery in Vornbach around the years 1173–1200. The municipal court of what is today Innstadt in Passau was assigned in 1258 to one Heinrich Razinger; thus he was "a high-ranking and evidently accomplished servant of the Prince-Bishop of Passau". Obviously the family at that time was well-to-do; in any case, one Otto Ratzinger was mentioned in 1318 as a citizen and homeowner in Innstadt (Passau). One of these two Ratzingers, according to Wurster, may have been the founder of the second Ratzing in what is today the district of Freinberg in Innviertel (today in Upper Austria), where he evidently acquired land and a country house. In any case, the local estate "Recing", later "Räzinger am untern Freinberg", is mentioned for the first time in 1304 in a document of the cathedral chapter in Passau. Thus on the Ratzinger estate developed the farming branch of a once bourgeois family that has been documented uninterruptedly from 1600 on. Since 1801, the family has owned the Strasser estate in Rickering, on which the grandfather of Benedict XVI was also born.

Father's father was also originally from Rickering, a hamlet that belongs to the parish in Schwanenkirchen. The oldest child of his parents was a girl by the name of Anna, who was born before their marriage. Then our father, Joseph Ratzinger, was born as their second child. He really never felt at ease there during his youth, because as the oldest son he had to help with the work on the farm at a very early age. That was difficult, hard work. Then he went to elementary school. At that time an assistant pastor by the name of Rosenberger taught there who played an important role in his life and made a deep, formative impression on him. He gave very intensive and valuable instruction in religion, which even then our father is said to have appreciated very much.

In addition he had a teacher, Herr Weber, who accepted children into the church choir at an early age. He led them in performing seven- or eight-part choral Masses, and our father was involved. Later, he liked to tell us over and over that even as a boy he had sung along in the church choir in Schwanenkirchen under the direction of Herr Weber. So early on, he was enthusiastic about church music, which apparently played an important role in the spiritual life of that parish.

During that time, our father developed his love for music. Then one day he bought himself a zither and took a few lessons; everything else he taught himself. In any event, he owned a whole box of sheet music that was always on the kitchen cupboard, right beside the zither. In the evening, then, he often took it down from there and played and sang for us. There was always a special mood when we gathered around him and he

played at first a stirring march and then some song from that
period. Today, probably, no one would understand those songs;
they were a bit maudlin and sentimental, but at the time they
moved us deeply. At any rate, it was always very nice when Father
played the zither, and it certainly predisposed me to embark on
my own career in music. Otherwise, Father was a strict but also
a very fair man. He always told us when something was wrong,
but he never scolded us unnecessarily and reprimanded us only
when we really deserved it. He certainly was a person to be
respected, even though he was always modest and friendly toward
everyone. He wore a handlebar mustache, as was the fashion
then, and was always impeccably dressed. For special occasions
Mother cleaned the helmet, saber, and belt of his policeman's
uniform very thoroughly with Sidol (*a cleaning solution*), for everything had to be bright and shiny.

After our father finished elementary school, he went on to
attend classes that were taught on holidays. These were for
former elementary school students who already had a job, like
Father, who long since had had to help at home with the
work on the farm. These classes always were held on Sundays,
and although other subjects were taught, too, religious instruction was central.

On October 20, 1897, at the age of twenty, he had to report
to the barracks in Passau and became a soldier. He was probably
a much better soldier than my brother and I ever were. He became
a noncommissioned officer and also wore the *Schützenschnur*, the
decoration for marksmanship, because he was a very good marks-
man, and he had also been recommended for this distinction by
his superiors. By no means did he consider his time in the military an unpleasant memory—unlike us; I must admit I was not
happy about being a soldier; nor was my brother. But my father
actually liked to reminisce about his time in the military. He
served for two years in the Sixteenth Royal Bavarian Infantry
Regiment in Passau and three more years in the reserves; then

he retired as a noncommissioned officer. He often told us stories from that time. For instance, there was one very vain Lieutenant von Hazy. When the commandant called him "Lieutenant Hazy", he did not move. Once again: "Lieutenant Hazy"; but nothing happened. But then when he said, "Lieutenant von Hazy", he would answer with a thunderous "Jawohl, Herr Hauptmann!"

After his time in the military, Father returned home at first. Soon it became clear, though, that, not he, but his young brother Anton would inherit his father's farm. Why that was so, Father never told us. He then had to decide what further career path to take, and he probably inquired about where he had the best chances with his training as a noncommissioned officer. They told him there were two possibilities, namely, with the police force, which at that time was called the rural police, or with the railroad company. I do not know what his reasons were at the time, but in any case he applied to the police force and was accepted.

The Bavarian State Archives in Munich still have on file his service record, which the local historian Johann Nußbaum from Rimsting found a few years ago. It states that he was "25 years old, Catholic, single, 5 feet 5 inches tall". His first assignment was in Niederambach near Schrobenhausen. After several transfers, he was appointed sergeant in Königssee after six and a half years, and eight and a half years after that, in 1917, he was promoted to a deputy constable in Kolbermoor, only two years later to constable in Unterneukirchen, then in 1921 to station chief. In thirty-five years of service, he was transferred fourteen times. "To outward appearances, he seemed lanky and tough. He wore a mustache that went gray early." So he is described by Nußbaum, who was able to speak with contemporary witnesses. "His demeanor was sober and stern. A robust man, modest and taciturn—typical for men from the region between the Danube and the Bavarian Forest."

At that time it was customary for policemen to be transferred often, if only to safeguard against any "special dealings". I certainly

Joseph Ratzinger, Sr., the Pope's father, as a young officer

cannot list all the posts to which he was assigned at one time or another. He was on Lake Königssee once, in Holledau, and during the First World War in Ingolstadt, where the local police unit was reinforced at the time, because there was a lot of industry there and the authorities feared an outbreak of riots among the workers.

The young policemen were poorly paid, and he probably said to himself that with those wages he could not feed a family. So he waited to marry until he was earning enough money. By then he was already forty-three. We never learned that he became acquainted with our mother by way of a personal announcement; he never told us that.

As was customary for policemen at the time, despite the fact that he was forty-three years old, he had to ask his superior first for permission to marry. Nußbaum found in the Bavarian State Archives the following letter also: "On November 9 (1920), I intend to marry the single cook Maria Peintner, born January 8, 1884, in Mühlbach, District of Rosenheim, and I hereby request the permission necessary to do so." After only one week he received permission.

Then there was the wedding. I think it took place in Pleiskirchen, where my sister and I then were born also. He lived there in a neighborhood called Klebing beside a little lake or pond, where the frogs were always croaking.

I visited Pleiskirchen for the first time a few years ago, thanks to arrangements made by one of our auxiliary bishops, Bishop Karl Flügel, who died in 2004. It is a pretty place with a very beautiful church and a castle with origins that go back to the eleventh century.

Nevertheless, our mother felt very uneasy in the house situated so remotely on the lake and was often afraid. That is why Father obtained a dog for her, but it proved to be even more timid than Mother, even though it was probably a very fine dog otherwise.

Generally those were troubled times. Inflation was raging then, prices soared immensely, and you paid as much as 200 million reichsmark for a loaf of bread. At that time my father was paid daily, but no sooner did he have his money in his hands than it was no longer worth anything, because the prices had gone up again. When I came into the world in 1924, Father later told me, my mother was very sick. She had almost not survived it. He himself was on an errand at the time, and when he came home I was already there in a basket, he said.

Yet there must have been beautiful moments, too, because our mother always used to say that the best time for her was when the children were still small. One year later, in May 1925, my father was then transferred to Marktl. That is where my brother, Joseph, was born.

The transfer document from the "Bavarian Rural Police Administration" dated April 22, 1925, is still preserved in the Bavarian State Archives.

Thereafter the station chief of police took up "his new position in the same service capacity with his previous basic wage as accounted for in the budget" on May 1. On November 1, 1927, Joseph Ratzinger, Sr., was then promoted "in the name of the government of the Free State of Bavaria" to security commissioner at salary level 6 with a yearly income of 2,124 reichsmark. As chief of the police station in Marktl, he was naturally one of the dignitaries of that locale, although he always conducted himself with reserve and modesty, as contemporaries testified. "In the relatively short time that he was here, he won for himself the respect of the inhabitants of Marktl by his sense of justice as well as his cooperation and friendliness in dealing with them", wrote the local newspaper, Der Burghauser Anzeiger *in 1929 upon his departure. Marktl am Inn, the* Süddeutsche Zeitung *said after the election of Joseph Ratzinger to the papacy, was located literally "between heaven and hell", that is to say, halfway between the Marian shrine in Altötting and the Austrian town of Braunau am Inn. There, on April 20, 1889, a man was born whose shadow soon loomed over the childhood of little Joseph and his brother, Georg: Adolf Hitler.*

If God speaks to us in history through signs, then perhaps also through this one: Marktl is 18.5 miles from Braunau; it is also 18.5 miles between Wadowice, the birthplace of Blessed John Paul II, and the concentration camp Auschwitz. Wadowice, too, had its nearby Marian shrine, the Kalwaria Zebrzydowska, only 12.5 miles away, with its "weeping" icon of the Mother of God. Both popes, therefore, were born in immediate proximity to places that symbolize, like no others, the rise and inhumane cruelty of National Socialism. Yet the two birthplaces are likewise under the protection of the Mother of God, who always vanquishes evil.

II
Marktl
(1925–1929)

M y earliest childhood memories come from the time when we lived in Marktl am Inn. The official residence of the policeman, thus of my father, was located there in a spacious house on the marketplace, the "Mauthaus", built in 1701. At the time of our move, I was a little more than one year old; my sister was already four. The central point of Marktl was and still is its church. Today only a part of it is preserved, since the church building from that time was partially incorporated into a new building that went up later.

The place of worship goes back to an endowment from the pious Berengar III Graf von Leonberg, who died in 1296. It was originally built entirely in the Gothic style and dedicated to Saint Oswald. After it was struck by lightning, the church and with it a large part of the village were destroyed by fire in 1701, but one year later reconstruction began. As the years went by, the newly constructed church became too small and was therefore torn down in 1853 and rebuilt. In 1964, there was a fourth building project, into which parts of the church from the nineteenth century were integrated, among them the neo-Gothic altar from 1857.

I can remember that it had an oratory, practically a rood loft on the side. From there Mother often pointed to the choir loft, where Father sang with the church choir. The pastor at that time was a Father Köppl; his assistant or vicar was one Josef Stangl, who is said to have been a rather strict man. Father Köppl,

Marktl am Inn around 1930

on the other hand, was charming and kind. He had a house-keeper named Olga, who owned a dog, to which I often brought bones that were left over from our meals. But the one person in all Marktl who impressed me the most was the town clerk, Andreas Eichner, who also signed my brother's birth certificate. In addition, he was the church musician; he played the organ, conducted the church choir, and on the side conducted a brass band as well. He was a short man, "Andresl", as we called him, but he became, so to speak, my first great model. He himself played the largest instrument, the tuba, and everyone used to say, "There is little Andresl with the big music!" We were well acquainted with him because our father sang with him in the choir. Of course at that time we children were still too young to go to church regularly, but often our parents did take us along.

With us in the house lived one of the first female dentists there ever was in Bavaria. Her name was Amelie Karl; she was single and had a traveling practice as a dentist. Probably the "Fräulein", as she was called, was the only one in the village to own such a newfangled motorcycle. When she drove off in the morning, it made a terrible racket that caused quite a sensation throughout the village.

In Marktl, our sister, Maria, went to school for the first time. There was an elementary school there that was located quite near our house. I always waited then for my sister, since now in the morning I was alone at home with Mother, who of course was busy with household chores or shopping. When Maria came home, we often quarreled but then made up again quickly, as children do. She was a very orderly person; with her everything always had its precise place, whereas I was a little genius of disorder. With me it seemed that chaos prevailed, but I always knew precisely where I had to reach when I needed something. My sister often straightened up my area and packed everything away nicely and neatly, and then I could not find anything anymore. So of course there was an argument. Yet that is often the case; girls are inclined to be clean and tidy, while boys are rather sloppy, and I was sloppy, I will be the first to admit it. But usually we got along well. A classmate of hers, whose name was Marei, died in the first or second grade, which at the time affected us children deeply. The story was that Marei had become seriously ill because she had always eaten snow. We were warned, therefore, not to eat any snow. I do not know whether there was any truth to it or whether it was just an old wives' tale.

One thing I still remember well is the attic of our house in Marktl. A lot of books were stored there—they must have belonged to a former resident—and they made me curious. So we always wanted to go up to the attic and at least look at the books, since we could not yet read. We discovered a drum up there, too, but I think our parents forbade us to play with it. In any case, I later got a drum for Christmas that particularly fascinated me. Whenever the sun shone on it, it magically produced different patterns on the drumhead. So there must have been something very special inside, I thought, and finally I poked through the drumhead. With that, the fine drum was broken, of course, and my first, still somewhat hesitant attempt to learn how to play a musical instrument had failed for the moment.

Then came the day about which so much has been written, that April 16, 1927, when my brother Joseph was born. It was Holy Saturday, and it is said to have been cold with a lot of snow—terrible weather, then. Yet all I remember is that I woke up and noticed that I was alone. Actually I was not used to sleeping alone; at that time my parents and my sister still slept beside me. But that night, or else in the early morning hours, I was suddenly lying alone in bed. No one had awakened me, as they usually did, and instead I heard the noise of hectic activity. Doors slammed, rapid footsteps resounded in the hall, people were talking loudly. When I heard my father's voice, I said, "Father, I want to get up!" But Father said, "No, you must wait a while; today we have a little baby boy!" At the time it was all a bit puzzling for me.

The future Pope Benedict XVI was born at 4:15 A.M., and his baptism followed that same morning at 8:30. Because the godmother, Anna Ratzinger, could not be notified quickly enough, a nun by the name of Adelma Rohrhirsch filled in for her.

In those days, the liturgy of the Easter Vigil was celebrated on the morning of Holy Saturday. Because the blessing of the baptismal water and the rite of baptism are an integral part of that liturgy, the parents did not hesitate long: "Well, the boy is already here now, so now he'll be baptized." In some way that was a special coincidence, a good omen. Only the other two children, Georg and Maria, had to remain back at the house, because it was snowing so heavily their parents feared that they might catch cold. The mother stayed home, too; she was still too exhausted by the birth to venture out into the snow. So the newborn, the first to be baptized with the holy water that had just been blessed, was christened "Joseph Aloisius". "On the threshold of Easter, but not yet through the door" (SE 42) became from then on the metaphor for his whole life, which from the very beginning was thus immersed in the Paschal mystery.

The neo-Gothic baptismal font, made of bright Danube limestone with six angels' heads, over which little Joseph Alois was held on that occasion has fortunately been preserved. It had been banished at first to the yard of the rectory when the church was rebuilt in 1965, and then the inhabitants of Marktl put it in their local museum in 1992. Research at that time found that it was the work of a sculptor in Munich, Anselm Sickinger (1807–1873), who had taken part in the construction of the Victory Gate in Munich. After the election of Joseph Ratzinger as pope, it "was allowed" to return to the church. Since then it stands before the neo-Gothic altar of Saint Oswald, a remnant from the former house of worship. On Easter Sunday 2006, which coincidentally fell on the Pope's birthday and the anniversary of his baptism, it was used again for the first time for the baptism of a child.

After a few days, I, too, was finally allowed to see my little brother Joseph. He was very slight and delicate. Father had hired a nun to help Mother during those days, because her health was still considerably impaired after the birth. This sister then tended, bathed, and dressed my brother. What worried us at the time was that when he was supposed to be fed, he could not keep his food down. She tried all sorts of things, but he did not like any of it, until the idea occurred to her to give him oatmeal. And lo and behold, he was able to keep the oatmeal down and even liked to eat it. It practically saved his life, for by then the sister was at a loss. Ever since, he has enjoyed oatmeal, as our father did, incidentally. My sister and I did not like it especially.

On other occasions, too, unfortunately, he was often sick. Once he even came down with a serious case of diphtheria, and then Father immediately called the doctor. It was a rather painful treatment; he screamed. On the day he came down with diphtheria, we were in our yard, where beautiful strawberries grew. Our landlord, the man who rented out the policeman's residence, had the fine name of Narrnhammer and was an awfully nice man. When he saw that we children were fascinated by the strawberries, he let us pick a few. My brother chose an especially pretty one for himself, but he was not able to swallow it, because his nose and throat were all swollen and inflamed by the disease. He may have been one or two years old, I no longer recall exactly.

At that time we had a good relationship with the owners of the house. Frau Narnhammer was a very cheerful person. I can still remember very well how she put her hands on her hips and laughed so loud that she roared. She had two daughters still at home. Often, when Mother was short on time, one of the two filled in and looked after us children.

Across from our house and to the left was a little convent of the Sisters of Mallersdorf. A Sister Pia lived there, whom I particularly respected. She later became the Mother Superior for awhile. A short distance outside the town, the sisters ran another house, Saint Anthony's House. Until a few years ago it was still owned by the order and served as a boarding school for homeless children.

Once the nuns reported to our father that someone was stealing from their garden regularly. They had a large garden in which they grew the fruit and vegetables they needed for the children's meals and their own. Father then tracked down the thief. In return, he received a big package from the convent, and Mother was very touched by all that was in it: sugar, flour, everything needed to feed a household. That was the convent's gift to thank him for catching the thief.

At that time in Marktl, there was Lechner's Kaufhaus, a grocery store that was practically across the street from our house. Today it is occupied by a pharmacy. During Advent, we—with my sister on the right, me on the left, and little Joseph, who could not yet walk by himself, in the middle—always used to go over to look at the display in the festively decorated shop window. There, surrounded by evergreen branches, gold foil, and tinsel, were toys that children might like to have. What fascinated Joseph most was a bear that had a very friendly expression. We went then every day, despite wind and weather, to visit the little bear, because we all liked it, but Joseph most of all had taken it to his heart. He would have liked so much to hold it in his arms. Once the owner of the shop, a very nice lady, asked us in and revealed to us the little bear's name: Teddy! Then one day, shortly before Christmas, we tried to visit the teddy bear again, but he was no longer there. My brother wept bitterly: "The little teddy bear is gone!" We tried to console him, but he was much too sad, and really we were, too. Then we went back home, quite disappointed.

Then came Christmas and the exchange of gifts. When Joseph came into the festively decorated room where the Christmas tree stood, he was so happy he laughed out loud. For there, where the presents for us children were set out, stood the teddy bear at his place. The Christ Child had brought it for him. That gave the youngster the greatest joy of his life.

Generally speaking, our family made a big thing of Christmas. The preparations already began with the First Sunday of Advent. At that time, the Rorate Masses were celebrated at six in the morning, and the priests wore white vestments. Normally violet is the color of the vestments in Advent, but these were special votive Masses that were supposed to recall the appearance of the Archangel Gabriel to the Mother of God and her words, "Behold the handmaid of the Lord, be it done to me according to thy word" (Lk 1:38). That was the main theme of these "liturgies of the angels", as they were also called, in which the appropriate passage from the Gospel of Luke was read. After we started school, we used to attend these Masses in the early morning, before classes began. Outside it was still night, everything was dark, and the people often shivered in the cold. Yet the warm glow of the sanctuary compensated for the early rising and the walk through snow and ice. The dark church was

Bernard Lechner's store in Marktl, where Joseph saw his first teddy bear

illuminated by candles and tapers, which were often brought by the faithful and provided not only light but also a little warmth. Afterward we went home first, ate breakfast, and only then set out for school. These Rorate Masses were wonderful signposts leading us to Christmas.

On the morning of December 24, we began first by putting together the family manger scene. Every year we were eager to make it even more beautiful. In 1929 we moved to Tittmoning, which was located on the Salzach, and along the river there were tuff stones that we used to collect. These are volcanic stones of several very different types: some had holes in them, others were grooved, while still others had bold, sharp corners, and with these one could decorate the crèche marvelously. We then brought a whole basketful of tuff stones and built wonderful hilly landscapes with them. (My brother still has the little family manger scene with the tuff stones from

Tittmoning; it is set up at Christmastime in the dining room of his apartment in the Apostolic Palace.) Then we obtained evergreen branches, which formed the background and contrasted nicely with the grayish stones, and scratched moss from the trees, which served as the pasture for the shepherds' flock. Thus our crèche took on a somewhat different appearance each year and was also expanded regularly. In some years, Mother bought additional figures, for instance, a few sheep or another shepherd and once even a sheepdog.

In the afternoon, our mother told us we should go for a walk. Usually there was deep snow, and then we went sledding, while Mother decorated the Christmas tree. Late in the afternoon we returned, and then we prayed the Rosary first. Praying the Rosary was a usual thing in our family, often daily, but at least every Saturday. We knelt down on the kitchen floor, each one with a chair in front of him, leaning his arms on the chair, and one of us, most often Father, led the prayers.

After the Rosary, we heard the sound of a bell ringing in the living room across the hall. There the Christmas tree stood, a little spruce tree, with the presents on the table. The sight of this, in the glow of candlelight, always made a deep impression on us. We used real candles that emitted a wonderful fragrance. The tree was ornamented with balls, angel's hair, and tinsel, and also with stars, hearts, and comets that our mother had cut out of bright yellow quince jam. Then Father read the Gospel to us, the Christmas story according to Luke, and we sang Christmas songs, "Silent Night", "Oh du fröhliche", and of course "O Come, Little Children". Once, in 1936, when I was already in high school, I myself wrote a little composition for Christmas. We three then performed it, my sister at the organ, my brother at the piano, and I with my violin. My mother was moved to tears, and even Father, although somewhat more level-headed, was impressed. From then on for a few years I regularly composed something at Christmas.

Because we were so impatient, the exchange of gifts always took place in our house a little earlier than in other families. There was always something wonderful about it, an almost fairy-tale quality to it. Of course we did not receive any magnificent gifts, but mainly things we needed, for instance, articles of cloth-ing, socks our mother had knitted for us herself, caps, or what-ever we happened to lack at the time. Moreover, each one also got a plate full of cookies and prunes, dried pears and fruitcake. These were wonderful things, and even today we remember them with great joy.

Of course we could all wish for something. I still recall what I received many years for Christmas. In 1933, when we were already living in Aschau, the Christ Child brought me a Fimoli-brand projector with which you could project whole series of pictures on the wall. In addition, I received three rolls of pic-tures, one about Altötting, one about the history of the ways in which the Cross has been depicted, and a third one about Rome. I was very happy with it. When the pastor heard about it, he asked me to illustrate with these photographs a lecture on Rome that he gave for the parishioners. In the Holy Year 1933–1934, he had ventured to make a pilgrimage to the Eternal City but of course had not taken photographs. That was not customary at the time, and so I as a ten-year-old showed pictures of the sights and the most significant churches, which otherwise he could only have described; this naturally caused something of a sensation.

In 1935, when I was in my first year at boarding school, I received a book of chant, the *Liber Usualis*, which was used at the seminary, and nevertheless, cost five reichsmark. It was a thick book with over a thousand pages, in which Latin text and the chant notation were printed. Joseph was quite impressed, because there was not a single German word in that thick book, but after all I was in secondary school by then and was already taking Latin classes. In my second year, I received the score to Rheinberger's Mass in F-minor, which we sang in the seminary choir, and in my third year, the piano arrangement of the beautiful composition "Das Lied von der Glocke", a setting by Andreas Romberg (*1767–1821*) of Friedrich Schiller's famous poem.

When we were younger, my brother, Joseph, usually received stuffed animals, and I got building blocks. So our wishes and talents were different. My brother received a second teddy bear, another time a horse, a duck, and a dog. He was very fond of animals, and therefore our parents always gave him stuffed animals. But once the Christ Child brought him a model train set, too.

Finally punch was served to us children, which of course was not very strong, and cookies, too. Afterward we had to go to bed rather early. When we were a little older, we woke up then at 11:00 in the evening so that we could attend Midnight Mass in the church. In the morning on the first day of Christmas, there was always a very special, festive breakfast with a Christmas stollen and pure coffee, which our father especially liked and to which he always looked forward. In the afternoon at 2:00, we attended Vespers, also; the church choir sang then, and it was always very solemn.

In our family, though, it was not only Christmas that was marked by the deep faith of our parents and the religious customs of our homeland. From our parents we learned what it means to have a firm grasp of faith in God. Every day we prayed together, and in fact before and after each meal (we ate our breakfast, dinner, and supper together). The main prayer time was after the midday dinner, when the particular concerns of the family were expressed. Part of it was the prayer to Saint Dismas, the "good thief", a former criminal who was crucified together with Jesus on Mount Calvary, repented on the cross, and begged the Lord for mercy. We prayed to him, the patron of repentant thieves, to protect Father from professional troubles.

Being a policeman, after all, was a rather dangerous profession, and we were often very anxious about Father. Especially

when he worked the night shift and had to walk the beat. When
a misdemeanor or a crime had occurred in the area he patrolled,
it was his duty to investigate it. Father often worked at night,
and then it could happen that he was held up, for whatever
reasons, and came home later. Then, naturally, we children and
Mother were anxious and prayed that nothing had happened to
him. So, of course, our prayer life was always marked by concern about Father. When we were children, our parents also put
us to bed and prayed our evening prayers with us. They used a
very special form of blessing and repeated it three times. Unfortunately I do not remember the wording today. This was followed by another somewhat expansive blessing. Once I asked
my father what it meant, but all he said to me was, "I do not
know exactly, either. My father and mother used to pray this
prayer at my bedside."

I must admit we seldom went to Mass together, simply because
our father had to work on Sunday or else sang in the church
choir. When we were somewhat older, I and then later my brother
served at the altar usually on Sundays and during the week, while
Mother and our sister went to another Mass. Often on Sundays
we attended Mass twice, once as servers and another time with
our family, for instance, the early Mass at 6:00 and the main
parish Mass at 8:00 or 8:30. Then, in the afternoon at 2:00,
there were devotions, and on feast days a Vespers service.

This piety, which was lived and put into practice, defined our
whole life, even though today I celebrate only one Mass and
refrain from going to a second one. Nevertheless, it was imparted
to us as children in the cradle, so to speak, and we remained
faithful to it throughout our lives.

I am convinced that the lack of this traditional piety in many
families is also a reason why there are too few priestly vocations
today. Many people in our time practice a form of atheism rather
than the Christian faith. In some respects, they may maintain a
sort of vestigial religiosity; perhaps they still go to Mass on the

major feast days, but this rudimentary faith long ago ceased to permeate their lives, and it has no bearing on their everyday routine. It starts with sitting down at table and beginning a meal without even thinking about prayer, and it ends with no longer coming to church regularly on Sundays. Thus, an almost pagan way of life has taken root. If there are no religious practices even in family life, then this has an effect on all the rest of human life. I often speak with brother priests, and in almost all cases it seems that they prayed regularly as a family and went to Mass together. This then shaped their whole lives and directed them toward God. Thus, their vocation fell on fertile soil.

In America there is a saying, "The family that prays together, stays together." In our time, when divorces are the order of the day, there are more and more broken marriages and single parents. Could this be because fewer and fewer families are willing to entrust their problems to God? Are families ruined also by a lack of faith and prayer? Do marriages fail because they leave no room for God?

I certainly think so. If you leave everything at the human level, then the decisive dimension where problems can be resolved is missing.

How did the Ratzinger family deal with marital and family quarrels?

We did not experience that, since each one settled that himself and with God in personal prayer. We did not talk about such things. There are problems in every family, and there were quite definitely in ours, too, but such problems became a part of our prayer. The personal concerns of each one of us were incorporated into that, and then we also surely found the solution there.

The story goes that the late Archbishop of Fulda, Johannes Dyba (*1929–2000*), came from a very temperamental family in which the members sometimes dealt with each other forcefully.

Yet after they went to confession, a very special peace returned to that family, and a special, conciliatory mood suddenly prevailed. Today, unfortunately, confession is much too often neglected, although it is, after all, the most generous offer of grace that God can possibly make us. We used to go to confession every month. When I was at the seminary in Traunstein, a Jesuit recommended that we should even confess once a week. I must honestly admit that we never did that consistently, but monthly confession is certainly right and necessary for everyone.

The course of the whole year was defined for us by the church holidays. In this regard, I should mention Easter in first place, naturally, even before Christmas. Throughout Lent there were "Mount of Olives" devotions, which in the city took place on Thursday, the day when Christ had prayed so desperately in the Garden of Gethsemane, but in the countryside were held on Sundays for practical reasons. They consisted of a rather long Lenten sermon and the devotion itself, which recalled the three falls of Christ: in Gethsemane, Jesus eventually fell to the ground three times, and so the Mount of Olives devotion was made up of three sections. First, the church choir sang. Usually a man sang a solo, and then there was a hymn and, finally, the prayer recited by the pastor, followed by a period of silence. In the midst of that silence, the large church bell then rang, which lent an especially impressive tone to the whole thing. In Dorfen, where I served for four years as an assistant pastor (*from 1953 to 1957*), there was a Baroque Mount of Olives. Christ was depicted as praying on it. During the devotion, the sacristan then used a crank to lower from the ceiling an angel that was hanging on a rope, with a chalice in his hand, so as to strengthen Jesus for his future suffering and death. Back then, in the Baroque period, as we know, they liked to stage things graphically like that. But sometimes it happened that the crank did not work, and the angel literally plummeted from heaven. But in spite of that, these

Mount of Olives devotions were always a beautiful and moving way to celebrate Lent.

The Easter Vigil ceremony, as I already mentioned, took place on the morning of Holy Saturday, together with the blessing of the baptismal water and the lighting of the Paschal candle. The celebration of the Resurrection followed that afternoon, another Baroque form of piety. At that time, in many churches, including the ones in Tittmoning and Aschau, there was a "Holy Sepulcher", in other words, an altar that was set up as Christ's tomb. On it the Most Blessed Sacrament was exposed, over which a white, transparent veil was placed. Beneath the altar, there was a statue of Christ lying in the tomb, adorned with flowers. Colorful, spherical glass containers filled with red, yellow, and green liquid served as special decorations. Thus the Holy Sepulcher offered a marvelous spectacle.

For the celebration of the Resurrection, the church was darkened; all the church windows were draped with black cloth. Then the pastor, in festive vestments and a cope, sang "Christ is risen" three times, to which the choir responded, the third time, "Alleluia!" Actually the priests are supposed to sing each time in a higher key, but most pastors could not distinguish the keys, since they were not that musical, either. Someone stood at each window to let the drapes fall as soon as the pastor intoned the third "Christ is risen." In Aschau, my brother and I did that, too, for a time. Then the spring sunshine poured into the church and created a Paschal mood. Finally, another procession took place, during which the church choir sang an Easter motet, for instance, in Traunstein, the "Attolite Portas" by Caspar Ett (1788–1847), a composer from Munich who worked at Saint Michael's. This procession with the Most Blessed Sacrament under the "heaven", as we called the baldachin, with lots of incense, was always a very festive occasion, which contributed to bringing the good news of the Resurrection deep into the hearts of the believers.

Besides that, there were other popular customs at Easter. There was the blessing of the foods that all the families brought with them, smoked meat or bacon, for example, salt and a few eggs; of course, decorating Easter eggs was also part of Easter. Mother and the ladies usually colored the Easter eggs with onion skin, which made them brown; that was the least expensive way of doing it. But there were also dyes at the grocery store that you could buy, so as to have very colorful Easter eggs. These were brought to be blessed, and of course the *Osterfladen*, a sort of braided yeast bread with a special glaze. Then we ate it after the ceremony. In addition, Mother always baked us a "Paschal Lamb" that was served to us for breakfast.

I have fond memories also of the May devotions that took place usually every day during the month of Mary. We always liked to go to them because the church was so festively decorated, with many flowers that enhanced the sanctuary not only visually but also with their beautiful fragrances. Then the church choir or a group of children sang.

In general, the Mother of God was always with us in our house. In our kitchen, for instance, a picture of Christ hung to the left of the crucifix and, on the other side, a picture of Mary. The Rosary, too, as I already mentioned, was prayed almost every day in our home. Only in the month of the Holy Rosary, October, did we go to pray the Rosary in church.

In those days, a special place in the church calendar was held by the feast of the Purification of the Blessed Virgin Mary, which was celebrated on February 2. Today, it is more a feast of our Lord, since it recalls the first visit of Jesus to his Father's house, his Presentation in the Temple. But back then, it was mainly a Marian feast. On that day, the family always prayed the Rosary with a special emphasis. Each one had a long, thin candle that he placed on the chair in front of him; we would light them and let them burn down during the recitation of the Rosary. In those days, people thought that the family member whose candle was extinguished first would also die first, but that of course was only a superstition.

Then there were the tapers; I still have a few today. The women often had a taper beside them in church, which they allowed to burn down during Mass. There were plain tapers but also those that were richly decorated. They played a very special role on the farms, where at that time there were still farmhands and maidservants. The maidservants had to take care of the farm-hands: they made their beds and darned their socks, and so on, and as a token of thanks a farmhand used to give to the maid who had served him a taper on the Feast of the Purification of the Blessed Virgin.

February 2 was also the so-called *schlankeltag* (from the Bavar-ian dialect word *schlankeln* = to move house), on which the hired help changed their place of residence. Whenever someone wanted to go somewhere else, the contract of employment always ended on the Purification of the Blessed Virgin Mary. That was the day when the domestic servants left their former employer and started a new job. So it was customary, here in Bavaria at least, for the farmer to ask the farmhands and maidservants ahead of time whether they wanted to stay on, and, if they were willing to do so, they received five marks on that day. In any case, it was an important day on the farmer's calendar and also a holiday on which there was no work. It always ended with a solemn Rosary in the evening with the wax candles.

Of course, we always celebrated our name days in a special way: Maria (September 12), Joseph (March 19), and Georg (April 23). On those occasions, there was always a particular tablecloth belonging to Mother, which I still have today. Every year on my name day, Frau Agnes Heindl, my housekeeper, brings it out again, the name-day tablecloth from back home. Early in the morning, a bit of pure coffee and a pie baked by Mother were served. Father also bought a bottle of wine to celebrate the day. Particularly in Aschau, when we were already somewhat older,

there were always two sorts of wine, either "Malaga" or "Samos".
Then we children, too, got a tiny little glass of "Malaga" or
"Samos" wine. Naturally on those days there was a festive meal,
and we got presents, too. Birthdays, on the other hand, were
not especially celebrated in our house; we only expressed
congratulations.

But now I have got far ahead of myself. Before we came to
Aschau in 1932, we moved first in 1929 from Marktl to Tittmoning, a small town that at the time particularly fascinated us.
We perceived Tittmoning, at any rate, as being very urban as
opposed to Marktl, which had a more rural character. It is a
pretty little provincial town, dominated by a large town square
in the southern style, around which small shops were crowded.
It was to be our home for the next three years.

III
Tittmoning
(1929–1932)

*T*he family's next stop, Tittmoning, is located on the Salzach, the river that forms the border between Bavaria and Austria. In his book Milestones, Joseph Ratzinger describes the provincial town as his "childhood's land of dreams" (M 10). He was impressed by the great town square with its elegant fountain, the town hall with its magnificent façade resplendent with portraits of Roman emperors in its niches, the huge old houses of the townsmen, the medieval city gates, and the defiant castle from the twelfth century, which sits enthroned on a height over the town and has served the bishops of Salzburg since the seventeenth century as their (seldom used) summer residence. He was impressed also, however, by its rich ecclesial history. Here the seventeenth-century mystic Bartholomäus Holzhauser not only recorded his visions about the end of the world, but also founded a charitable institution, a residential association for secular priests. Since then the pastor has been called the "Dean" of the foundation, the assistants were "canons", and the rectory was enthroned like a pretty little castle at the highest point of the town.

The police force and, therefore, the Ratzingers were accommodated in one of the most beautiful houses of the historical town, the so-called Stubenrauchhaus. It was located right on the town square and once belonged to a charitable institution. Today a plaque at Wägnergasse 3 recalls the famous family's stay, whereas the building now houses the local bank. Its impressive façade with the beautiful bay window at least temporarily caused the family to overlook the fact that their domicile was in rather poor condition. But that did not matter to the children. They found all that exciting and mysterious and felt as though they were in an old knight's castle.

Tittmoning had a thoroughly Salzburgian character. After all, it was once an establishment of the bishops of Salzburg and to a great extent owed its former wealth to the earlier salt trade. The house in which we lived once belonged to the cathedral chapter of Salzburg. There we had a very large room that once served as the chapter meeting hall. This apartment, however, was rather impractical. The stone floor was full of cracks; the creaking wooden stairs were steep and inconvenient. Even the heating proved to be quite troublesome, since the fuel for the wood and coal stove had to be brought up by that narrow, steep stairway. It soon became too much of a strain for our mother to be constantly carrying heavy wicker baskets up the stairs, and so one day she ordered from the basket weaver a *tragekraxn*, a hamper with straps that you could carry on your back. In the summer, fortunately, there was no need to heat, and so she just had to transport the firewood for the cooking stove, but in the winter, fetching wood became real drudgery. Downstairs in the house there was a shop where utensils, horseshoes, nails, and all sorts of things were sold. The landlord was a certain Herr Stubenrauch; he was a peculiar man. He was probably hard of hearing; at any rate, you always had to speak very loudly until he understood something. He had a maid who now and then came to Father in tears to report the landlord. Then our father had to call him to order in due season. Later on, I again met this maid, whose name was Rosa; she worked at first as a maid at the seminary in Traunstein. During the war, she again crossed paths with me. I was serving at that time in various parishes around Traunstein as an assistant organist, and she had meanwhile been employed as the housekeeper of a pastor in the vicinity of Traunstein.

Tittmoning had a night watchman; I was afraid of him at first. We were unacquainted with that in Marktl. So we were awakened at night, my brother and I, because he sang so loudly:

The siblings Maria, Joseph, and Georg Ratzinger

Hört ihr Leut' und lasst euch sagen,
Uns're Uhr hat zwölf geschlagen.
(Hear ye, people, what I tell:
Our town clock has now struck twelve.)

Then I said to my parents, since we were all sleeping in the one big room, "There is a wicked man outside shouting; what is the matter?" Then my parents had to calm me first and explain that he was the night watchman, who sees to it that nothing happens.

Generally it was a very romantic little town. When I think of Tittmoning, the first thing that occurs to me is a very beautiful collegiate church that had a considerable fascination for us even as children. In it the faithful revere an image of the suffering Christ that is painted in such a way that you have the impression the eyes are following you. Then there was the convent chapel, which was also the school chapel, in which Masses for the school were held. In the convent chapel there was a sodality that held solemn devotions with a procession every month. During this procession, there were always two boys who carried a *stäbchen*, a small pole with their spiritual emblem. Then I, too, became a staff-bearer and was very proud of it. For this purpose we received a white cowl with a leather strap as a belt, and then we boys were allowed to walk along in the monthly processions in the church. My mother always used to go to this devotion with my brother and sister just to see me in the procession.

Then in Tittmoning there was a splendid shrine church, the Ponlach Chapel, which is officially called Maria Brunn zu Ponlach and is situated somewhat above the town. Tittmoning is framed, so to speak, on one side by a flat mountain, or better, a hill. On it is located a big, imposing castle that was later used as a country boarding school. But at that time we were more interested in and liked very much the Ponlach shrine, which is located quite close to the castle. We often went with Mother to this bright, friendly little Rococo church. It stood in the middle of the woods, over a ravine, and the rushing water of the Ponlach made such a beautiful sound there. I have a wonderful memory of this magnificent church and then the rushing stream in the wooded ravine through which we so liked to walk.

The late-Baroque central structure of the shrine church with the front steps and niches where spring water flowed was dedicated in 1717. Even at that time a statue of Mary made out of linden wood attracted pilgrims. The miraculous image was produced by a sculptor from Salzburg, Hans Pernegger, in the years 1639–1640, in the midst of the Thirty Years' War. Only later was the Blessed Mother clothed in a festive garment. The side altars of the chapel are decorated with figures by a sculptor from Tittmoning, Johann Georg Itzlfeldner, and the ceiling is painted with four scenes from the life of Mary. Over the choir loft, nine frescos refer to Marian shrines all over Europe, while an inscription tells:

> *Maria Plain, / der Trost allgemein;*
> *(Alt-)Oetting reich an / Gnad für jedermann;*

Allzeit Ettal / ein Gnadensaal;
Hilf zu Passau / bringt die Schutzfrau;
Maria Zell / beschützt Leib und Seel;
Maria Schnee / bringt Trost im Weh;
Loretto floriert / vom Himmel ziert;
Einsiedeln weicht, / von Gott selbst geweiht;
Monserat fruet / die ganze Christenheit.
(Maria Plain—a consolation for all;
[Alt-]Oetting is rich in grace for everyone;
In every season Ettal is an abode of graces;
At Passau the Protectress offers help;
Maria Zell protects body and soul;
Mary of the Snow brings comfort in woe;
Loreto is in flower, adorned by heaven;
Einsiedeln retreats, consecrated by God himself;
Montserrat gives joy to all Christendom.)

In the Ponlach rift valley, which has an abundance of springs, the stream flows through the shady glen over a series of little waterfalls.

Then there was a so-called *bienenheim*, a little park where the citizens could keep their bees and through which Mother liked to walk with us. Then she sat down on a bench and did her needlework while we played, and so she spent the afternoon with us. Another spot where we liked to spend our free time was, of all places, the prison in Tittmoning. It was part of the girls' school that Maria was attending, and along its back wall there were benches set up, to which we were drawn on many a summer day. The town square in Tittmoning was framed by two old city gates, the Burghauser-Tor and the Laufener-Tor. If you walked through the Laufener-Tor, you came at first to the train station. When a train arrived with its locomotive, it resounded mightily and kicked up dust and soot. From there you could travel from Tittmoning to Wiesmühl an der Alz, and we often made a day trip to that town. But then, behind the train station, you arrived at the cemetery with its beautiful chapel, which we often went out to see. Out there, close to the cemetery, lived a man who owned a harmonium. His name was Max Auer, but we called him "Auer Maxl", and he gladly showed his harmonium to anyone who came to visit him. So I always used to beg Mother, "Can't we go to Auer Maxl's house and look at his harmonium?" Then we did, and he even let me work the keys on his instrument. The sounds that I produced with two fingers were not very artistic.

Tittmoning had a port suburb. The city itself is situated somewhat on an elevation, but the port suburb is located lower down, right at the bridge over the Salzach. The river was also the border with Austria. There was a toll booth there, and ten pence was collected from everyone who went over the bridge, and then we were abroad. Of course that fascinated us to no end. Our mother got along well with the wife of the border official, and so there was always a little snack before we continued our trip to Austria.

The first place on the other bank of the Salzach was called Ostermiething. On that street, a blacksmith had his workshop. When my brother was still very little, he once asked loudly, "Is that a blacksmith?" From inside resounded the answer, "Nope, a gingerbread baker." Evidently he was a man with a good sense of humor. Not far from the border, to the north of Ostermiething, there was another little town by the name of Sankt Radegund, in honor of Saint Radegund, who had a very interesting life story.

The Thuringian princess Radegund (518–587) was taken hostage along with her brother after the victory of the Merovingian King Clotaire I over her father and brought to the Frankish royal court. There she received baptism. After the death of the queen, Clotaire forced Radegund to marry him. Once she was married, she wanted to devote herself to a life of penance and charitable work instead, which repeatedly led to conflicts

with her husband, the king. After her brother was murdered, she took
refuge with the Bishop of Noyon, who consecrated her a religious. In
560 she founded a convent in Poitiers, which she herself entered as a
simple nun. Soon women from all over the empire followed her example
and wanted to become nuns, too. Even the Byzantine emperor heard
about the pious former queen and in 569 sent to her a relic of the true
Cross, which is why she renamed her convent Sainte-Croix.

There in Sankt Radegund they regularly performed Passion plays,
which I attended together with our mother. Another time we
saw in an open-air theater in Tittmoning a performance of *Andreas
Hofer*. Generally we loved the theater. A friend of ours even had
a marionette theater, which little Joseph in particular enjoyed
very much.

Tittmoning was really romantic, I must say. Above all, the city
square was a magnificent sight during the Advent season, if it
snowed then, too, just because the display windows of the shops
were so festively decorated. In Marktl, there was only one shop
that had a display with a Christmas theme, the Kaufhaus Lechner mentioned before. But in Tittmoning, they were lined up
one after the other. The house next door to us belonged to the
Pustet bookshop. That is an old family of booksellers going back
to Friedrich Pustet (*1798–1882*), who was originally from Passau and later settled in Regensburg. He founded a publishing
house and bookstores in many cities, not only in Bavaria, but
actually all over the world. His nephew Anton, in turn, founded
the Verlag Anton Pustet, a publishing house in Salzburg. And
then there was the Pustet bookstore right by us in Tittmoning,
which always had a wonderful display that was decorated very
beautifully at Christmastime.

Generally books played an important role in our family. Our
mother always told us about what she had just read. She liked
novels best, for instance, on historical themes like the Fuggers
[an influential merchant family]—a fine book that I still own

Tittmoning, city square—historic postcard. At the left front, with the bay window, the Stubenrauchhaus, in which the Ratzinger family lived

today—but also romantic stories. I remember, for instance, a novel with the title *Roma, the Pearl of the Eternal City*, by Kurt Allmendinger, that was published in 1930. Just at that time I was taking first-year Latin in school and supposed that Roma was the name of the city of Rome, but in the novel it was also a woman's name. She told us wonderful stories about it, including spiritual stories, since the books she read were usually by popular Catholic authors. Father, then, especially on Saturdays, read "the Goffiné", as people used to call the masterpiece by Father Leonhard Goffiné (*1648–1719*), the *Christkatholische Handpostille* (Catholic handbook of prayers). The book contained the readings at Mass for Sundays and holy days, but it also explained them quite well and related them to themes from everyday spirituality. Father frequently read to us from it. And then, of course, there was the *Schott*, named after its publisher, the Benedictine priest Anselm Schott (*1843–1896*), who in 1884 published the first "Missal for Laymen". Since then his name has become synonymous in German with all sorts of missals for the laity. When we were little, we had a children's missal, a little book with pictures and tiny captions that explained the sequence of sacred actions, so that we could follow what was happening at the altar quite well. Later we received a *Schott* for children, which contained the essential texts of the liturgy. We then studied it diligently. My parents, of course, owned the real *Schott*, which their pastor had given to them for their wedding in 1920. Thus we were introduced step by step into the mystery of the liturgy, about which we became more and more enthusiastic as we matured.

In Tittmoning, "life began to get serious" for us brothers in the fall of 1930. I started elementary school as a six-year-old, while my brother continued to go to the kindergarten in the basement of the Augustinian convent. The *Kinderbewahranstalt* (child-care center), as it was called then, was run by the religious order of the Englische Fräulein (English ladies). It was directed by Sister Maria Korbiniana Kreuzburg, a small but energetic nun.

Earlier I liked going to kindergarten, but my brother at first did not like it at all; he would have preferred to stay home with Mother. Only later was he quite happy to go to kindergarten. When he came home one day, it had obviously made a powerful impression on him. On the feast of Saint Nicholas (*December 6*), not only Saint Nicholas came to visit, but also Krampus, his wicked attendant. Of course the sisters used this pedagogically and staged it accordingly. He really pounded on the door and made a racket, and two auxiliary sisters had to hold the door closed so he could not come in. Then she told the children who this Krampus was, and that they must prevent him from doing them any harm. With that, they gave the children a healthy fear of the Evil One.

Yet what sounds like a childhood idyll—and probably was one, too— was soon disturbed by the events of that time. Poverty and unemployment did not stop at Tittmoning, and here, too, the political climate became noticeably more intense. There were constant elections; the city was plastered with garish posters and pithy slogans; and some political gatherings degenerated into riots. Again and again, the father of the Ratzinger family had to intervene as a policeman. In particular the NSDAP, the National Socialist German Workers' Party [the Nazis], proved to be a constant cause of unrest, always ready to resort to violence. They intentionally incited people so as to pose as the only alternative to the threatening chaos.

I can still remember well that at that time there were walls for posters in Tittmoning, which were used by various parties for their propaganda and to invite people to political gatherings and rallies. As a policeman, my father of course always had to be present, as things were often very heated and sometimes also quite dangerous. He always used to tell about it when he came back home; of course we never experienced it firsthand.

Five-year-old Joseph and his brother sensed that their father was increasingly worried about the future. Adolf Hitler, the self-appointed savior of the Nazi Party, was utterly repugnant to that devoutly Catholic man. Instead, the police officer was an enthusiastic reader of the newspaper Der gerade Weg *(The straight path), which had become the mouthpiece of politically involved Catholicism. The editor-in-chief of the paper, Doctor Fritz Michael Gerlich, did not mince words where Hitler was concerned. "National Socialism is a plague", he started one editorial on July 31, 1932, only to predict prophetically: "National Socialism, however, means: hostility toward neighboring countries, tyranny at home, civil war, international war. National Socialism means lying, hatred, fratricide, and boundless misery. Adolf Hitler proclaims the law of the lie. You who have fallen for the deception of a man obsessed with tyranny, awake! Germany, your fate and the fate of your children are at stake!" After the party seized power, the editor who had courageously warned his readers had to pay for such great candor with his life. Storm Troopers (SA-Männer) beat him almost to death in his office, only to arrest him afterward. For fifteen months they held him in prison and tortured him; then he was brought to the concentration camp in Dachau and murdered there.*

I am not sure whether Father subscribed to it, but I remember clearly that *Der gerade Weg* was often in our family's house and was very much appreciated. Father spoke with us very little about politics at that time, for he knew the proverb: "Children and fools speak the truth." He feared that we might blurt something out that could be detrimental to him and us. Our mother said a little more; she was more open in that regard. At any rate, our parents made no secret of the fact that they were anti-Nazi and despised Hitler wholeheartedly. In any case, they admired Fritz Michael Gerlich for his courage.

My father, of course, read *Der gerade Weg* because it spoke to his soul, as it were. Besides that, he subscribed to the *Münchner Tagblatt*, which reflected somewhat the views of the Bavarian People's Party (BVP). At the time, that was the Catholic party here in Bavaria, which especially in the countryside was the strongest opponent of the NSDAP. After the Nazis seized power, unfortunately, it was forcibly dissolved.

The Church, too, at that time took a public stance against the Hitler movement. As early as October 1930, the Vatican newspaper L'Osservatore Romano explained in a front-page article that membership in the NSDAP "could not be reconciled with a Catholic conscience". The Archbishop of Munich, Michael Cardinal von Faulhaber, used even clearer words and characterized the National Socialist ideology as a "heresy"—as blasphemous heterodoxy. It was "strictly forbidden" for Catholic clergymen to support the Nazis in any way whatsoever. After a series of identically worded instructions at the diocesan level, the German Bishops' Conference in August 1932 issued uniform guidelines for dealing with National Socialism. The party platform of the NSDAP was declared "heretical", the "anti-Catholic character" of the Brownshirt Movement was publicly denounced. Catholics were forbidden to

*belong to the Party; anyone who disobeyed this directive was as a rule
excluded from the sacraments. Catholicism and National Socialism were
thus clearly irreconcilable.*

Our path, on the other hand, led in quite a different direction.
Music fascinated me from the beginning, especially church music.
It began in Marktl, when Andresl was my great example, and
continued in Tittmoning when I met Auer Maxl with his harmonium. In church I saw a clergyman who was active as an
organist and a layman who conducted the church choir. So I
became extremely interested in church music and was captivated
by it. Luckily my parents supported my inclinations from the
start. As our stay in Tittmoning was coming to an end, my father
learned through a newspaper advertisement that a used harmonium was being sold somewhere. It cost—I still remember
precisely—241 reichsmark and was soon afterward delivered to
our new address in Aschau. That is how my music career began,
which eventually led to a position as cathedral choirmaster. Once
I asked Father what the word was for the man who conducted
the choir in the bishop's church. Father answered that he was
called the cathedral choirmaster. "Then someday I will be a cathedral choirmaster", I told him. Later doubts came. But at the
time, when I was so young and naïve, I was sure about it. Just as
my brother, back then in Tittmoning, was quite certain that he
would become a cardinal someday. That was of course, to put it
quite bluntly, nothing but childish prattle. We had no idea that
one day it would come about exactly as we had said.

At that time Cardinal Faulhaber, the Archbishop of Munich
and Freising, came to Tittmoning to celebrate the sacrament of
confirmation.[1] He was an impressive figure and arrived in a black
limousine, the likes of which did not exist in Tittmoning. We

---

[1] According to the records of Cardinal Faulhaber preserved in the archives of the Archdiocese of Munich, this was on June 19, 1931; Joseph Ratzinger was four years old at the
time.

At the photographer's studio, the Ratzinger siblings appear in their best Sunday clothes: to the right, with a ball in his hand like an imperial orb, the future Pope

Joseph Ratzinger (circled) in the kindergarten in Tittmoning

had never seen such a fine automobile as the Cardinal's. The driver stopped, and the door did not open until Father, as the police officer of the place, who on this occasion wore his freshly cleaned uniform with polished saber, helmet, and belt, finally opened it wide. Then the Cardinal climbed out with great dignity and surveyed the crowd with a majestic glance. That made an extraordinary impression on us all, while my brother laconically noted, "I'll be a cardinal someday!"

A few days later, our apartment was painted. The painter did the job so skillfully that my brother at first watched, utterly fascinated, and then announced to us: "I'll be a painter someday, too." Of course those two professional goals were somewhat far removed from each other. But he still had all the time in the world to make up his mind about his vocation.

IV

Aschau

(1932–1937)

Even during the pre-Nazi period, our father had already taken on the Storm Troopers, broken up meetings, and thereby identified himself politically as a blunt anti-Nazi, which was generally known in Tittmoning. He did not talk much about it with his family, probably intentionally, so as to protect us. Then, as it became clear that the Nazis were going to come into power, his superior advised him to leave Tittmoning, because it could become dangerous for him there. So after serving there for only three years, he requested a transfer from the rural town to a village and came to Aschau.

In mid-December 1932, shortly before Christmas and only six weeks before Adolf Hitler seized power, the five-member family moved. Aschau am Inn, their new home, is described by Joseph Ratzinger in his memoirs as "a well-to-do agricultural village consisting of large, imposing farms. . . . In the middle of the village, as is always the case in Bavaria, there was a large brewery whose restaurant was the meeting place for the men on Sundays. The actual village square was at the other end of the place, with yet another nice restaurant, a church, and a school" (M 13). Their new residence was a modern house, by the standards in those days, with a bay window and balcony, which a wealthy farmer had built and now rented to the police. The future pope, in any case, regarded it as "a cozy home" (M 13).

Aschau was a long, drawn-out place, a so-called *strassendorf* (street-village), and our house was located more toward the far end,

Aschau, Dorfstraße; to the far right, the residence of the Ratzinger family

away from the church. It was a nice two-family house, "a real villa", as Mother said the moment she saw it. Father's office, which he shared with an assistant, was on the ground floor along with the latter's apartment, while we lived in the floor above. People came to the office and filed reports, against a neighbor or whomever. There was also a telephone there, as in Tittmoning, but we were not allowed to touch it; it was strictly for business. At that point in time, we ourselves did not yet have our own telephone. The house had a beautiful bay window that we immediately liked very much. Then on the first story [above the ground floor] there was a kitchen-dining room with a stove and the table at which we ate meals. Besides that, there was a sofa or a "canapé", as people used to say then. The harmonium, too, which was delivered soon after we moved in, had its place here. On the other side was the living room, which was very nicely furnished, although in the winter it was rarely heated. Then there was a bedroom in which Father slept with us boys and a second bedroom for Mother and our sister. In a hall that connected the rooms with each other, we set up the Christmas crib immediately after we moved in. We very quickly felt at home there. A small addition to the house accommodated the holding cell. The delinquents whom Father had apprehended had to stay overnight there until he or his second-in-command brought them the next morning on foot to the jail in Mühldorf, which was ten and a half miles away. Since the policeman also had to provide board for the fellows who were arrested, Mother shared our food with them. So they had the best possible care, since she was always a very good cook.

In addition, the house had a beautiful garden, which of course gave Mother great joy. In that garden there was a little pool of water that served as a carp pond. In it my brother almost drowned once. This pond was located at the foot of a small slope, which Joseph at that time in his childish exuberance used to slide down, until he fell in the water and was in danger of perishing. Luckily my parents reacted quickly enough, grabbed him, pulled him out, and thus saved his life. The fishpond was filled in soon after that, and today no one remembers exactly where it was located. When my brother became pope, I was invited to Aschau for the unveiling of a memorial that had been set up in his honor. I spoke then with the mayor, a very friendly man, who could no longer even remember there had ever been a pond there.

The general store was located not far from the church. There were several shops in the village, but this one was the most important. It belonged to a Frau Bastl, who had several children, and one of her sons was in my grade one year. The shop had everything the heart could desire: groceries and sweets, bonbons and chocolate, pencils and penholders, paper, fabrics for aprons, and clothing for Mother and our sister, really everything. For us it was a veritable fairy-tale kingdom. At the other end of the village was the Thann hamlet. There a studious young man lived, Franz Xaver Kronberger (*1913–2010*), who had just earned his secondary school diploma (*Abitur*). I still remember how he used to wear the *Abitur* cap with a red velvet ribbon on which the *Abitur* badge was printed, the *Abiturzipfel*, a triangular piece of cloth that was worn on one's pocket watch, and the white-and-red *Abiturband*. We were immensely impressed by that at the time. Later he studied theology and became an assistant pastor at the cathedral in Munich. We met him again then, and a good personal relationship developed.

The most important man in Aschau was of course the pastor. Our pastor, whose name was Alois Igl, had a beneficiary by the name of Georg Rinser, an uncle of the author Luise Rinser. Frau Rinser may have been somewhat eccentric, but her uncle was an awfully nice man. He was a bit handicapped, mentally as well as physically, for he had once been stung by hornets and became so seriously ill afterward that he had to go on disability. He had a housekeeper named Elis (which sounded somewhat more dignified than the usual "Lisl"), who always gave us something when we came by, for example, a nut or whatever. She simply needed to do something nice to everyone who visited her, and for that reason alone we always liked to go to her house.

Other dignitaries in Aschau were the secondary school principal and the teachers, some wealthy farmers, some of whom unfortunately soon proved to be inveterate Nazis, and then of course the policeman, our father. People had a proper respect for him back then. They used to tell the little ones that the policeman would punish naughty children, although of course he was concerned only about adults who had committed punishable offenses.

A real one-of-a-kind character was Andreas Brand. Besides his occupation as a barber, he was also a clockmaker, electrician, insurance agent, gas station owner, and photographer. He took the first photos of us children. When he disappeared behind his gigantic apparatus, we always heard him say, "Keep still, now!" but at first something always went wrong. He was somewhat slow and rather taciturn besides, but he was always able to take care of himself somehow and eventually managed in every situation. Somewhere along the line, in 1934 or 1935, we then bought a very simple camera of our own, a Kodak camera that cost three or four and a half marks. We were immensely proud of that camera, even though, naturally, it could not take photos as good as the ones Brand took in his studio. Later the Americans took the camera with them when they were occupying our house near Traunstein in 1945, which made us very sad at the time.

Next door to us was the Ametsbichler brewery; they were the wealthiest family in that place. They had five children; the older, Thomas, was already at boarding school; the second, who was also named Georg, was in my class; the fourth, Bärbel, was exactly as old as my brother and attended the same class with him in 1933. Since they walked the same path to school, they went to school together and probably also befriended each other. Other than that, we boys at that age did not have much contact with girls. Boys just have a different temperament. Even in the classrooms, boys and girls sat separately; on the left side, the girls; on the right side, the boys. As a result, there were simply more friendships among us boys, and the girls likewise kept to themselves. It was similar in our family. At first Maria and I were the older ones, and we two stood opposite to my brother. Later, though, we two boys stuck together and our sister became more attached to Mother. In any case, she could tell good stories and always reported to us in detail what she had experienced at school. Being younger, we always listened attentively, since we wanted to know what was ahead of us when it was our turn to go to school. Yet we practically never played together as a threesome.

As brothers, Joseph and I were one heart and one soul. Naturally we also quarreled and fought, that is part of it, but by and large we were inseparable, and that remained so our whole life long.

Were you well-behaved boys or real Bavarian rascals?

I think we were somewhere in the middle! We were not especially well-behaved, that was clear. I would say that my brother was somewhat better behaved than I. But we were not real rascals, either, who started all sorts of trouble; you cannot say that.

What trouble did those boys start, then?

Well, on the other side of our house lived a small farmer who owned an oxcart. He always walked five paces ahead of the team and called back, "Vee-ah!" Do you know the commands used to drive cattle? At the sound of "vee-ah!" they started off; at "hü!" they stopped; at "hott", they turned right; and at "wüst", they turned left. He always used to call "vee-ah!" and "hü" but did not even turn around when he did so. So it often happened that "wicked" schoolboys secretly stopped the oxcart so the farmer arrived home all alone. Suddenly the cart was no longer behind him!

Life in Aschau was naturally quite different from our time in the city, in Tittmoning, which had more of an urban character. But that really did not interest us very much. We did go regularly into the fields, for instance, in the spring to pick lamb's lettuce, but otherwise we had relatively little to do with farming. It was already clear to both of us that our vocation was in an entirely different field and that Aschau was only an intermediate station along that path.

A very likable saint, Konrad von Parzham (1818–1894) lived during the nineteenth century. After working for years as a farmer, at the age of

thirty-one he entered the Capuchin monastery of Altötting, and he served
there for the rest of his life as porter. He practiced sacrificial love by his
willingness to help everyone who asked him for counsel and help. Nei-
ther age nor sickness kept him from performing his duties eighteen hours
a day. Finally, though, when he was utterly exhausted and near death,
he asked his superior to relieve him, and he died three days later. Pope
Pius XI, who beatified Brother Konrad in 1930 and canonized him in
1934, explained: "In him shine forth purity and humility, love for
God and neighbor, fidelity to duty"—duties that impressed young Joseph
Ratzinger, also. So even later he often asked himself how it was that
God shows himself most clearly in simple people. That also became for
him an incentive never to forget his own roots and never to "stand out"
intellectually.

I still remember well the beatification of Brother Konrad in 1934
on May 20 (Pentecost), for which we of course made another pilgrimage to Altötting. We three children stood there with our
mother and watched endless crowds of people file past us in the
solemn candlelight procession, fervently praying, "O Mary, help
me, O Mary do help me, a poor sinner implores you." For me
as a youngster, only ten years old, that seemed somewhat tiresome, but nevertheless I found it very impressive to see so many
people, all of them holding candles in their hands and calling on
the Mother of God.

The monastery church fascinated me, too, especially the Chapel
of Grace, the gallery of which was covered from top to bottom
with votive plaques donated by people who had implored the
Blessed Virgin in times of great need and received help from
her. They were for us a visible sign of the miracles that took
place there, the fact that the Mother of God works even in this
world and has delivered people from their troubles and problems. In those days, people still made their way along that gallery on their knees while praying the Rosary. So we knew that
those people had a serious concern or an important petition and

were entrusting themselves confidently to Mary's protection and help. The penitential practice of praying on their knees served to make reparation and to intensify their prayer.

But the day of the canonization, of course, was centered on Brother Konrad. We children really did not know much about him, only that he was a very good man who got to heaven because he was so kind and led a faith-filled Christian life. Even that impressed us and incited us to follow his example. It was good to know that right nearby a man once lived who now was surely in heaven with the dear Lord and could serve as an example for us.

But it was also a dramatic day. On that occasion we had a bowl of soup for lunch in the convent of the "English Ladies", and there was a wasp or a bee in it that stung my brother on the eye. My brother has an allergic reaction to bee venom. His eye was badly swollen, as a result and he suffered for the rest of the day of the canonization from the consequences of that sting.

In Altötting I began to become interested in the stands where you could buy devotional objects. Many nice little things were offered there that we boys could use while playing pastor, for example, little monstrances, miniature chalices, candlesticks, and many other things, and of course candles, too, in all possible shapes and sizes. My brother and I enjoyed playing at being priests. In Catholic families in those days, it was a popular children's game, which of course had the additional purpose of preparing boys to serve at the altar and perhaps even for a later vocation to the priesthood. Children's altars with little chalices, monstrances, and so on, could be bought then in any toy store, and of course we had one, too, although ours was built by our Uncle Benno from Rimsting. It was a really beautiful high altar, which he even equipped with a rotating tabernacle. The preparation of the gifts took place with little cruets and chalices made of tin. Naturally we used water instead of wine for the make-believe consecration. We also had a censer, which often got tangled up when it was swung, and even Mass vestments that had been made by the seamstress who sewed clothing for our mother and sister. Her name was Wally Kifinger, and she lived on the other side of the Aschau stream that ran through the whole place. You arrived at her house by way of a narrow footbridge. She had an invalid sister by the name of Fanny, who lived in her house and for decades had been confined to bed. As an altar server, I went every day with the pastor over the narrow footbridge to Wally's house to bring Communion to her sister. The pastor made these sick calls in a cassock with a stole and ciborium, and I walked ahead with a bell in my hand and rang it. The people whom we met along the way knelt down and made the sign of the cross, for they knew we were carrying the Blessed Sacrament with us. Every day we went to see her, whether it was summer or winter. In winter the footbridge was usually iced over, and so it was not such a simple matter. Most of the people in Aschau were deeply religious Catholics. There were also several sodalities that celebrated their feast days splendidly.

There was much excitement in our house shortly after we moved in, when the harmonium that our father had bought was delivered to Aschau. I can still remember well that wonderful instrument. It had thirteen registers, including an unusual one: an *Äolsharfe* [Aeolian harp], which is a 2′ stop in the bass; the registers are called 8′, 16′, and 4′, corresponding to the respective octaves of the pitches they produce. We were all tremendously impressed by it all, but of course we could not yet play music. And so Father then went to the pastor and asked him whether he knew of a teacher for us, that is, for my sister and me at first. He knew of no one except his lyceum student Else Pölzl. At that time a lyceum was a sort of a secondary school for older daughters, which was attended by girls from the better families after they had completed elementary school. Else gave each of us a half-hour lesson once a week, so that we at least learned the basics, for she did not know much about music, either. In return, she then received a certain amount of pocket money from Father. Her sister Hilde, incidentally, was in the same class as our sister. She later married and had five sons, three of whom joined the Regensburger Domspatzen. I am still in contact with them today.

My career as a church musician began quite unexpectedly. This is how it happened. Our teacher was also our organist and church music director, but he was also a Nazi through and through. It went so far that often he even came to school in his brown shirt. Later, during the war, he was drafted and fell in action. At any rate, one day he was no longer willing to play the organ in church on weekdays. He said that it could not be done; the "Führer" did not want it; he had to be in the school. But since we had a school Mass every morning, our pastor did not want the children to have to do without music entirely, either. So he bought a harmonium and asked me whether I could play. I felt I had in the meantime mastered the instrument sufficiently to accompany the hymns the children sang, and so I gladly accepted the invitation. That was in 1934, and I was ten years old at the time. Back then I would bring the sheet music from the organ to use. One day, though, the music book was not in its place, and I wondered what I could do; I finally decided to play the hymns from memory. Later, the pastor, who knew something about music, said that everything had gone right. I must say I was just a bit proud of the fact that I as a ten-year-old at the time could accompany the hymns without a hymnal. It was not even difficult for me, and my mother was very happy, whereas my father, a rather sober fellow, said nothing, which was just like him, though.

The chronicle of the parish in Aschau notes on December 20, 1934: "A fifth-grade pupil", meaning Georg Ratzinger, "splendidly accompanied the German sung Mass and the Latin choral Mass."

Later my brother, Joseph, had harmonium lessons, too. At that time my sister was already attending a domestic-help school in the convent in Au. It was a school where girls could learn many practical skills, from stenography, bookkeeping, and typing to home economics. Therefore, we were well acquainted with the sisters in that convent, and each week our mother brought Joseph to one of them, who was instructing Maria to play the harmonium. He then had his harmonium lessons with the sister at the convent.

Later, at the seminary, he also learned how to play the piano. Of course, the piano is the real keyboard instrument, and the harmonium is only a poor imitation of the organ, and anyone who wants to accomplish something on a keyboard instrument should first know how to play the piano. Yet in our case the sequence was just a little different. Not until my parents moved in 1937 to Traunstein did we find out that there at the outskirts of the town stood a house of the "English Ladies" where used pianos were sold. Then Father bought us a piano, too, and we were able to take piano lessons.

As cathedral choirmaster-emeritus, what is your opinion of the Holy Father's musical talent?

I admit that it was easier for me, yet he was certainly musical and also enjoyed music and was very adept at playing. After all, it takes brains, too. He promptly learned to read music; he understood a piece of music very quickly, a process in which his intellectual receptivity and his ability to react rapidly were a great advantage. Still, he did not take to music quite as spontaneously as I did. I always loved music passionately. In this respect, he was a little more restrained, although he is a very musical person.

In any event, transporting his piano from his cardinalatial residence to the Apostolic Palace in 2005 caused the moving crew considerable headaches.

That's right. Today, though, it stands in the papal apartment in the living room, which is right next to the dining room.

Does he play regularly?

Rarely, he says. But usually he opens the hymnal. Max Eham, the cathedral choirmaster in Freising, who then became cathedral choirmaster in Munich, wrote a lot of hymn settings at that time for the seminary choir in Freising and compiled them later into a little hymnal that my brother still has today. It is often lying on the piano, and he plays the most common hymns from it. But occasionally there is "more difficult" piano literature on the music stand. Unfortunately, he plays less now since he broke his hand (*on June 17, 2009*), he says. Then, too, with age your fingers naturally become stiffer. I notice, too, how my ability to play has diminished over the years.

The rural idyll, the seemingly carefree existence of the Ratzinger broth-ers was deceptive. The dark shadows of politics did not stop at the entrance to the village of Aschau. On January 30, 1933, President Hindenburg transferred the office of chancellor of the Reich to Adolf Hitler, which was celebrated by the Nazis as their "seizure of power". "And that is exactly what it was, too", Joseph Ratzinger explained later in his memoir, Milestones, *"From the first instant power was exercised" (M 14).*

We had been living for just six weeks in Aschau when it was announced that Hitler had been elected. Most people were shocked. Yet it was decreed that the whole elementary school would process through Aschau; practically speaking, they orga-nized a demonstration or a parade for the "Führer". So we walked through the village and then back again. It rained in torrents that day, and we marched bravely through the puddles, which in itself was rather ridiculous.

Our father was very angry and of course also very worried about this development. From our parents we children knew only that Hitler was very wicked, a thoroughly evil criminal, and that *Hitlerei*, as they called National Socialism, was a bad thing—but not much more than that. The people in the village reacted in various ways. Those who until then had not dared to show their sympathy for the brown "pied-pipers" now appeared publicly as Nazis, whereas others tried to cope somehow with the new reality. A few Nazis started up a local branch and, of course, pressured our father to become a member of the NSDAP. Then Father said that under no circumstances whatsoever would he join the Party, but so as not to put our family completely at risk, he advised Mother to join the women's organization. It was headed by Frau A.,[1] a very pious lady who used to pray the Rosary while walking down the street. She even held the Rosary in her hand when she made the Hitler salute! Our mother then told us about what went on at the meetings of the National Socialist Women's Organization in Aschau. In fact, they did not talk about Hitler but instead exchanged recipes, chatted about their gardens, and sometimes even prayed the Rosary together. Of course that was a rather atypical "Nazi" gathering that had nothing at all to do with the Brownshirt ideology.

The assistant policeman, Herr W., while not a Party member, was nevertheless very ambitious. One day he heard that another day of recollection was going to be held in the church. He hoped he could blacken the reputation of the priest from Gars who was supposed to come and preach on that occasion. For at that time, a policeman received a decoration if he informed on a priest. So he went into the church with a notepad, hoping the priest would say something against the Nazis that he could then

---

[1] In order to protect the descendants of the persons in question, Msgr. Ratzinger asked that their names be concealed.

report and thus score points and further his career. But the pastor had learned that W. intended to take notes and warned the priest not to preach under any circumstances. Instead, since it was Lent, he took the opportunity to make the Stations of the Cross with the people who went to church. Then the assistant policeman, instead of taking notes, had to kneel down and stand up again fourteen times. The people, of course, knew he had come for another reason and grinned with *schadenfreude* to see him "on bended knee".

Joseph Ratzinger, Sr., reacted to the seizure of power in 1933 in his own unique rational, logical way. "Now war is coming; now we need a house!" he announced to his family. That same year, he purchased with his savings—a total of 5,500 reichsmark—an old, run-down farmhouse (built in 1726) in Hufschlag near Traunstein, to which the family was to move after his retirement.

Shortly thereafter, Joseph started school. A class photo from that time shows him in the third row, slightly bent over, with a somewhat skeptical look. In the background stands an instructress looking sternly at them, and on the blackboard one can see the results of the first arithmetic assignment: 1 + 1 = 2. The first attempts at writing had already been made also: the blackboard reads "Au meine Nase" (Ow, my nose). On the wall hangs a crucifix, and beside it two photos. They show President Hindenburg—and alongside, Adolf Hitler.

People in the village were still divided. At first, most of the inhabitants of Aschau had a wait-and-see attitude toward the new government. Thus, Joseph Ratzinger recalls, for instance, the battle that was sparked in 1933 over denominational schools. Until then the "Catholic elementary school" was the common model: the pastor or the assistant pastor was also the religion teacher and taught the catechism in religion classes. The Nazis wanted to cut off this connection. The schools were to be subordinate to the State alone and would no longer communicate the Christian faith but, rather, the ideology of the "Führer". In order to placate the Church, Hitler offered a concordat immediately after seizing

Aschau, 1933: Joseph Ratzinger in the first grade (third row, second from the right)

power—in other words, a fundamental agreement that supposedly would secure the Church's rights. The bishops hoped thereby to prevent the worst from happening and were at first willing to deal with the regime. They did not suspect that the new government never had any intention to abide by existing agreements. Only when it was much too late did the bishops attempt in their pastoral letters to exhort Catholics to break the law. Uselessly, as it turned out.

Only a few of Joseph's teachers were really rooted in the faith. Many older teachers had their own grievances against the Church and had felt they were being led by the nose with the previous clerical supervision over the schools. In the younger generation, there were many convinced Nazis. One of them even tried to redesign village life, which was traditionally shaped by the Church's liturgical calendar. He organized solstice celebrations and explained that it was high time to turn to sacred nature and one's own ethnic heritage instead of continuing to believe in sin and redemption. Those were all foreign, Jewish ideas that were only imposed on our Germanic ancestors by the Romans who occupied the

Joseph Ratzinger's First Holy Communion in 1936; he is in the first row, the second boy from the left

land. Now, though, it was important to free oneself from the yoke of this foreign religion. On May 1, he had a Maypole set up with great pomp. In a "prayer" that he himself had composed, he praised it as a "symbol of a life force perpetually renewing itself" (M 16). It was supposed to help reestablish a bit of Germanic religion and drive out Christianity. Yet the indigenous farmers who lived in Aschau just smirked. And the village youths were more interested in the sausages that hung on the Maypole and were to belong to the fastest climber.

Nevertheless, politics did not stop even at the door to the elementary school. So Joseph had to take a stand early on and defend what he believed in. His strict religious upbringing contributed to the fact that he never had problems keeping his distance from the brown spook.

As Joseph Ratzinger was preparing for his First Communion in 1934, his father bought him his own Schott, the missal that translated into German the prayers of the Mass, which were still in Latin then. Consequently the book, which was published in a handy popular edition, became his guide through the mysterious world of the liturgy, which at the time

The Ratzinger family around 1937

was still celebrated in Latin. Understanding it was for the staunchly Catholic youth a veritable voyage of discovery. "To move forward into that mysterious world is always something beautiful for a child and a young person", he said later about his enthusiasm. "In this way love for the liturgy has its roots in this event, and consequently what is alive in the real centerpiece of the Church of course also grows very early on—precisely as an answer to fantasies and dreams as well" (L).

So it was only logical that one day Joseph wanted not only to follow what was happening at the altar but to become part of it. "Not to be there yourself, you would have felt somehow excluded from what was most important", (L) he admitted—and he became an altar server, like his brother before him.

At some time or other a lighthouse was set up on the Winterberg in the immediate vicinity of Aschau. At night when it patrolled the skies with its glaring light, it appeared to be summer lightning foreboding an uncertain danger. Soon people were saying they could sight enemy aircraft that way. But until then, there had been no airplanes at all over Aschau, much less those of an enemy. Something sinister was in the air like a front of dark clouds on the horizon. We had a premonition that something was being prepared that no one in the village wanted to admit was true. Maybe Father was in fact right, and the Nazis wanted war.

V

Traunstein

(1937–1946)

E ver since Hitler seized power, our father had been anxiously looking forward to his retirement, for it was profoundly repugnant to him to serve an executive branch of government made up of criminals. He would have preferred to retire early; after all, he had sworn his oath of office to the king and not, as he put it, to a *stromer*, an evil scoundrel. But then he held out after all, as difficult as it was for him, because at that time all officials who remained in service until their retirement date received a settlement of several thousand marks, which our family bank account of course needed urgently. He even took sick leave for awhile and used the time for extended hikes with Joseph, the only one who was still living with our parents. At that time, I was already in boarding school, at the Archdiocesan Minor Seminary of Saint Michael in Traunstein. Then my brother would always say, "Father, tell a story", and our father, who was a gifted storyteller, began an impromptu story. These tales always began with the words, "A husband and a wife lived in ..." and took place somewhere in the Bavarian Forest.

Then, on March 6, 1937, the policeman had finally reached his sixtieth birthday and could go into retirement. The family moved to Huf-schlag bei Traunstein, into the old farmhouse he had bought after the Nazis seized power. They arrived there in a borrowed automobile. It was spring, early April, and the meadow in front of the house was strewn with primroses. The house itself was very simple. The roof was still covered with wooden shingles that were weighed down with stones so they would not be blown away by the wind. There was no running water; fresh water had to be fetched from the well. In hot summers it happened now and then that it dried up completely. Yet despite this, it seemed to the ten-year-old Joseph like a paradise "beyond our wildest dreams" (M 22). He found all that highly romantic, adventuresome, and mysterious. Right behind the plot of land the woods began, and in the morning when the curtains to the bedroom window were opened, Traunstein's two "local" mountains, the Hochfelln and the Hochgern, seemed close enough to touch. Joseph was happy, although he was now at home without his siblings. In the abandoned shed on the property, he could pursue his daydreams but, above all, read, and read a great deal. His first writing attempts also date back to this period. He composed a whole series of romantic poems about nature and everyday life. During the holidays and on weekends, his brother returned from boarding school, and the boys played ball together on the meadow in front of the shed or gathered berries in the forest and wood for the heating stove.

It was a very old farmhouse; on one of the beams you could still read the year in which it had been built, namely, 1726. The front part was the living quarters, while in the back there was a stall and rooms in which to store wood and hay. When you entered the house, on the right was the combination living room and kitchen with the stove at which Mother cooked, the couch, and the table at which we always sat. When the war began, my father bought a radio, for it was clear to him that the Nazis were really just lying to us. He wanted to know what was actually happening. With the radio, which also was in the kitchen, he could receive foreign stations; that was actually a punishable offense, but he did not care. More important to me, on the other hand, was the fact that one could also listen to music on the radio, which at the time interested me much more. Besides, our father was not the only one who thought that way. At the beginning of the war, he was recalled to active duty and therefore had to go back to work as a policeman; a colleague asked him then whether he would listen to the PTT, too. That was a Swiss station, which of course was always quite neutral and objective in its reporting. Later he used to listen also to French and English military stations, which for propaganda reasons alone transmitted German-language programs. Anyone who was not a staunch Nazi listened to these stations, although it was strictly forbidden. Naturally, you always made sure no one heard anything about it and put the radio on very low so that it was unobtrusive, because there were a lot of informers. Reception was always poor because the Nazis did everything they could to block the transmissions. But it simply was not worthwhile to listen to German stations, which merely spread Nazi propaganda. "The only thing on them that is true is the time and maybe also the weather", my father used to say.

The house stood in the middle of our plot of land, which was a good day's work, in other words, covered about five-sixths of an acre. There was a large garden in front and another garden just as large behind the house. In front of the house, mother had planted an herb and vegetable garden, in which she herself grew the most essential things we needed: beans, lettuce, radishes, even strawberries, but also flowers, which she loved so much. The birds loved them, too, and so we always had a birdhouse in which she hung a cake of suet and strewed bird food so they had provisions in winter. In addition, a few fruit trees grew in front of the house: one apple tree had tiny little apples that tasted excellent, however, and then there was a pear tree, and finally, behind the house, there were also plum and cherry trees. Also a meadow that Father always used to mow. During the war, when there was nothing to eat, he fed a sheep with the hay. Later he sold the hay so as to add a bit to the family's cash on hand. To store the hay we had a separate hayloft. We boys were often up there, and the pussycat we had in Traunstein felt very much at home there, too.

One book maintained that we secretly smoked up there, but that is not true. My brother never smoked, and I did exactly twice in my life: when I was released from the labor service, the unspoken rule was that every man had to have smoked, and so I smoked, too, in order to try it. Then during our theology studies, there was a Professor Johann Auer, who taught us dogmatics and the history of dogma. Once when it was his name day, the feast of Saint John the Baptist (*June 24*), we sang him a serenade, and then he gave each of us a cigarette, which we were supposed to smoke. I immediately had a coughing fit, and since I already coughed so much anyway, I certainly did not need to smoke as well. On the other hand, our father liked to smoke; he loved "Virginia cigars". Of course he did not indulge in smoking during his working hours but, rather, in the evening, when he had free time. He could smoke one cigar for days; over and over, he would put it out and light it again, so as to enjoy it for as long a time as possible. A Virginia cigar was of course expensive, and so he had to divide it up. But we brothers never smoked.

The house in Traunstein was really a home for us, a little paradise. We had just moved in when we experienced the *Georgi-Ritt* (George's ride), which is still carried out on Easter Monday in honor of Saint George. The whole city was on its feet. Previously a group had performed a medieval sword dance on the city square, and then began the actual ride up to the little church in Ettendorf. Ettendorf is the next locality over from Hufschlag and is located perhaps ten minutes away. The mayor and the local pastor usually rode in a coach, although there were also clerics who rode on horseback like the rest. It was very festive and a great event for the whole city. Several hundred splendidly decorated horses and just as many riders participated in those days.

In Traunstein, which even today he calls his real "hometown", a new phase of life began for the ten-year-old Joseph Ratzinger, also. He now started the first year at the "humanistic" gymnasium, the secondary school that offered classical languages. It now took him a half hour to walk to school, but that did not bother him at all, for now at least he had "ample time for looking about and reflecting, but also for reviewing what I had learned in school" (M 22). The instruction in Latin suited him. For the rest of his life he would be grateful that he had learned the language of the Church "with old-fashioned rigor and thoroughness" (M 23), for later as a theologian he could read source material from almost two thousand years of Church history in the original texts. Greek, the language in which the New Testament was originally composed, was also in the curriculum. These two ancient languages became his favorite subjects.

What he liked even better was the fact that at the gymnasium in Traunstein, National Socialism had not yet gained any more of a foothold than it had at the primary school in Aschau. Now he witnessed twice the firing of the headmaster because he would not say what the Party wanted to hear. Somehow he had the impression that a classical education and grappling with the intellectual world of antiquity made a person immune to the delusions of the Brownshirts. When the music teacher opened the songbook, in which there were a lot of classics along with the Nazi songs, he immediately told his students to cross out the words "Juda den Tod" (Death to Judah = the Jews) and to replace them with "Wende die Not" (dispel our plight). But after only one year, even this island of intellectual freedom was flooded. By law, all the gymnasiums *in the Reich were combined with the science schools into a so-called* Oberschule *[generic high school]. Greek instruction disappeared completely from the curriculum, Latin was cut back substantially and was offered only from the third year on. Modern languages and the natural sciences were stressed more instead. With the new type of school came a new generation of teachers to the school, almost all of whom were decided Nazis. Soon religious instruction was totally banned from the curriculum, and the quota of physical education classes was increased accordingly (see M 23–24).*

I can no longer say exactly when I first heard the call to the priesthood, for actually it had always been clear to me that that was where my destiny lay. When I was an altar boy and served Mass, I already knew that that would be my place: now I was an acolyte, but later I myself would have the privilege of standing in the priest's place. I never doubted it for a moment; it all happened naturally, in an almost organic development. I never really had to think about it, so sure was I of my vocation.

Of course, it is a different situation with every priest. I know, for example, a pastor who had already started a career when a First Mass was celebrated in his hometown. Initially he did not want to attend, but he was actually compelled to participate in that first Holy Mass of a young priest. At first, he stood way in the back of the church; then he was pushed farther and farther toward the front by the crowd, until, at the end of the Mass, he was standing almost right before the altar. At that moment he realized he belonged there, and he decided to become a priest.

Here there is simply no "golden rule", no set prescription. I, at any rate, never had to wrestle with myself and did not need to make a difficult decision. Actually it was clear to me from the beginning—although serving at the altar and, of course, perhaps more than anything else, the spirituality of our family had something to do with it—that I would go into ministry. For me, that was always something self-evident.

I do not know whether I was consequently an example to my brother in a certain way. At least he saw in me what that life could be like, when he himself decided to follow me on that path. We never talked about it directly, but I can well imagine it may have encouraged him a bit at least or confirmed him in his decision. Of course the anti-Christian spirit of the times strengthened our resolve to follow that path "now more than ever", with all its consequences, and to remain true to our vocation, come what may.

In any case, I went to the Archdiocesan Minor Seminary already in 1935, when we were still living in Aschau. Since the seminary did not offer its own classroom instruction, we went from

Rather hesitantly integrated into the community: Joseph Ratzinger ca. 1940 on a school outing (middle row, fourth from the left)

there to the humanistic *gymnasium* in Traunstein. Joseph came to the same *gymnasium* in 1937, but for two years he still lived at home, until in 1939 he likewise entered the seminary. My brother was the last one in a *gymnasium* class; the next class after his already belonged to the government-run high school.

To start with, there were thirty-eight of us children in the *sexta* (the first *gymnasium* class), thirty-five boys and three girls who were all Evangelical Lutheran. At that time most people in our region were simple craftsmen or farmers, for whom it was simply not customary to send a daughter for higher education. Moreover, most of the teachers were older gentlemen and accordingly had conservative opinions and were often religious as well; there were no female teachers yet at our *gymnasium* back then. Only later did a few younger teachers arrive, who brought a different mentality into the school, and among them there were also fanatical Nazis. One of them was, for instance, our new headmaster, after his predecessor had died of pneumonia. Still, most of them were not, and they maintained good relations with the seminary as well.

The academic year was divided then into trimesters, not into semesters like today. It began with Easter. The Easter holidays were followed by three months of school, then a long break for summer vacation, which we called the "major holidays", and in September it continued until the Christmas holidays, when the second trimester ended and after which the third began. Only later was the beginning of the school year moved to the fall.

At the beginning of each trimester, a flag-raising ceremony took place. For this occasion, the whole school had to line up in formation; then the temporary headmaster gave an inflammatory Nazi speech, and finally the flag was hoisted. At that, the school music teacher intoned the German national anthem, which we were all supposed to sing in chorus. Of course there was something unintentionally comical about the way he first gave the "German salute" and then with his outstretched hand set the tempo and conducted, while a youth hoisted the flag of the German Reich. At the end of the trimester, the flag was then taken down again. The provisional headmaster, Herr K., was also our mathematics teacher. He was a short Saarlander with a big paunch. Therefore we used to call him "Kelly-belly". He was actually a believing Christian but at the same time a decided Nazi; how he was able to combine the two I do not know to this day. At any rate, the flag-raising was followed by the salute to the Führer, during which he regularly got mixed up. He used to say, "To our much loved, ardently loved, cordially loved Führer Adolf *Sieg*, aaah, no, well … to our cordially loved, ardently loved Führer Adolf *Sieg*. . . ." Of course, he was supposed to say: "Adolf Hitler: *Sieg Heil!*" but somehow he never managed to say that; he always pronounced only the words "Adolf *Sieg*", and we could hardly keep from laughing.

Later on, when I had already left the school, some Nazi big-wig or other often came from the provincial leadership in Munich and regularly scolded the conservative *gymnasium*, which must have been very unpleasant.

At the *gymnasium*, naturally, I had Latin classes, and one of our teachers was a philologist of ancient languages, Doctor K. His son became a priest and for a long time was pastor in Trostberg. At any rate, this Doctor K. liked to talk an especially enthusiastic brand of politics, and we took advantage of it. Someone always used to ask him how the war was going, and he began to hold forth; a torrent of words just poured out of him. Of course we did that, not out of any interest in politics, but only so that Latin class would go by faster and he would no longer have time to ask us questions about our homework.

Then came Saturday. Originally we had Saturdays off from school, but soon they introduced a new subject called "N.G."— *Nazionalsozialistisches Gedankengut* (Nazi ideology), and, of all days, it was scheduled for that day. For this class one of our teachers had to speak about a Nazi topic. I still remember well one of our teachers, Herr Fauner from Amberg, who was a brave, conservative man and had little interest in the Nazis. When it was his turn, he gave a talk on the VDA, the Verein für das Deutschtum im Ausland, the "League for German Culture Abroad", a German academic association to which he belonged. It had been founded long before in 1908 and naturally had nothing to do with the Nazis. Another teacher always used to tell about the First World War, and each of his lectures ended with him quoting Herrn von Schlieffen (*Alfred Graf von Schlieffen, 1833–1913, General Field Marshal and General Chief of Staff of the German Empire*), who had worked out the battle plan for the First World War and even on his deathbed declared, "Strengthen the right flank for me!" That was the lesson, and afterward we also went to the athletic field and had to play at a sport, because we were all supposed to get fit for war.

My brother was a first-class student from the beginning, much better than I ever was. When I had already been drafted into military service, in 1942, Mother once wrote to me that he was one of the top three students in the *gymnasium*. It was just that "calisthenics", as we called physical education classes then, did not suit him at all; he was a poor athlete and not good at drawing, either—art class used to be called "drawing" then. That made him "only" the third best student, whereas in the humanities and the sciences he was always the best.

To be honest, we detested sports. Our father always used to tell about his time as a soldier in Passau, in which he had to do physical exercises and let his head roll around over his shoulders. He always used to say, "As farmers we have so much work and can never keep up with it all, and here I am in Passau rotating my head!" That alone took the enjoyment out of sports for us. To be sure, neither of us was very gifted in that area, either, but there was also this innate dislike, a regular aversion to it.

In early 1939, the pastor in Haslach, Stefan Blum (who made the circuit of several churches, including Hufschlag) recommended that the twelve-year-old Joseph, too, should enter the Archdiocesan Minor Seminary so as to have a really systematic introduction to the spiritual life. Joseph was enthusiastic about the idea. His brother, who had already been at the boarding school for four years, had told him only good things about it, and he had already made friends with a few seminarians. For his parents, however, it was not an easy decision, for it meant an additional financial sacrifice. His father's pension was rather meager, and so his mother now had to take a job during the holiday season as a cook at a hotel in Reit im Winkl so as to earn something more. His sister, though, after receiving her diploma and doing the year of service in agriculture that was obligatory for girls at the time, had taken an office job in a big company in Traunstein and thus eased the family budget somewhat. Through these common acts of self-denial, Joseph Ratzinger remarked later, the family also developed an "inner solidarity . . . that bound us deeply together" (SE 44). Thus, sacrifice brought them all together, and right after Easter 1939, at the beginning of the new school year on April 16, the younger son, too, was able to enter Saint Michael's Archdiocesan Minor Seminary, which had been founded ten years before by Cardinal Faulhaber.

In the recommendation letter that Herr Ratzinger submitted to the minor seminary on March 4, 1939, Hubert Pöhlein, the assistant head-master at the Traunstein gymnasium, praised young Joseph as a "well-behaved, diligent, and reliable" student. The physician Doctor Paul Keller emphasized in his medical certificate that "the boy's digestion and physical strength" had "improved": although moderately under-weight, the lad was in the best of health. Joseph had passed the entrance examination with a grade of "1" in religion, "1–2" in reading, "1" in language, "2" in spelling, and "1" in essay-writing. Because Herr Rat-zinger had painstakingly calculated that he could raise only 700 reichsmark per year for his two sons—his monthly pension was 242 reichsmark—the tuition was set at that precise amount.

Of course it was not so uncommon for two sons from the same family to intend to become priests at the same time. I know several examples that I have encountered during my career, for instance, the former pastor of Saint Francis Church in Munich, Hans Wammerdinger, who was originally from Wasserburg, where his father used to deliver bread; his brother likewise became a priest. I remember, too, how our seminary choir was once asked to substitute and to sing in Saint Oswald parish in the city of Traunstein, because the parish choir was in Anger that Sunday, where two brothers were celebrating their First Mass together. So it was not that unusual at all for several boys in a family to become priests and the daughters, nuns. Nevertheless, it was of course something of a burden for our parents. That is why our mother occasionally went to Reit im Winkl to work there as a cook during the tourist season and to earn additional money. She used to send me off, saying, "Take good care of Joseph", because the whole situation at boarding school was something rather new and unfamiliar to him.

It had not bothered me in the least; I actually felt at home from the very beginning at boarding school. Things did not suit Joseph so well, however; it is more accurate to say that he did not like it at all. But he himself says today that it did him good, because if he had always stayed at home, he would quickly have become a loner. To be sure, in community he had to pay a price that did not suit him, but he did become acquainted with community life and was thereby equipped with social skills he might otherwise have developed only with difficulty.

That was to date the most profound upheaval in his life. The young Joseph Ratzinger had to understand that he was one of those people who is simply not made for life at a boarding school. "While at home I had lived and studied with great freedom, as I wished, and had built a childhood world of my own", Cardinal Ratzinger explained in Milestones. *"Now I had to sit in a study hall with about sixty other boys, and this was such a torture to me that studying, which had always come so easily to me, now appeared almost impossible" (M 25). Even more drastic for that freedom-loving individualist was the experience of suddenly having to share a dormitory with forty boys. "For me that was an unprecedented restriction, in which I suddenly had to fit into a system. It was extraordinarily difficult for me", he admitted (L).*

The daily routine was strictly regulated. We used to rise at 5:20 A.M., even though that is unimaginable today. Then we washed and dressed and prepared for Mass, which began at 5:40. The whole seminary participated in it.

At that time the priests celebrated facing the high altar. The marvelous painting over the high altar, a depiction of our Lord being taken down from the Cross, was unfortunately damaged recently in a fire. Then there were also two side altars. Five priests staffed the seminary, namely, the rector, the three prefects, and the spiritual director. So besides the Mass at the high altar, Masses could be celebrated at the two side altars, also. The Masses took a rather long time, because in those days practically every seminarian went to Holy Communion.

Mass was followed by early morning study until 7:10, then breakfast. After breakfast we had to pack our schoolbags, and at 7:30 we lined up for our walk to school. Punctually at 7:35, the whole seminary, all nine classes, walked in two files down to the school, which began at 8:00.

After school came the midday meal, after which we had to go to the playing field, which I never really felt very inclined to do. There various games were played. Soccer was forbidden; instead we played handball, dodge-ball, *treibball*,[1] and other ball games.

At 3:00 in the afternoon, study hall began, which was interrupted at 4:00 by a coffee break—coffee was served with a roll. At 4:55, the college preparatory courses began, and the evening meal was at 7:00. After that we finally had free time: usually we played billiards and board games in the study hall, but sometimes we also read books.

At 8:05 P.M., we had spiritual reading, and, at 8:20, evening prayer in the chapel, where we all gathered again. That was always very moving—the almost dark chapel filled with the students' prayers. At the conclusion of evening prayer, one of the prefects went to the front and blessed the whole community. Afterward we observed strict silence and went to the dormitories. These were large rooms with forty-two beds. This, too, is unimaginable today, but at the time we thought nothing of it. Two students from the upper grades also slept in the dormitories for the lower grades in case something happened and someone needed help. During the night a small, dark red light always burned.

---

[1] *Treibball* is a game in which two teams try to drive each other back by throwing a heavy ball as far as possible over a line in the middle of the playing field.—TRANS.

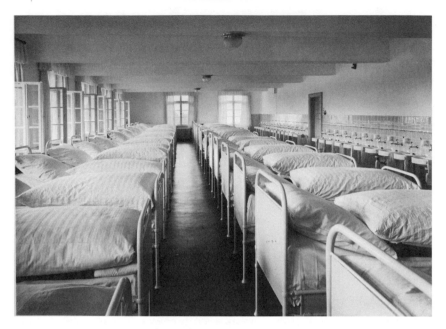

The dormitory was for Joseph Ratzinger an "unprecedented confinement"

Everyone had a locker in the corridor and his own desk in the study hall and, besides that, a closet compartment in which we could store the foods we had received from home. So in the early years, my brother, when he came from home, always brought along the sandwich Mother had prepared for me for the coffee break.

As I said, all these things did not bother me, and I made many friends in the seminary. But for my brother it was something of a trial. At any rate, we seminarians were a close-knit community at the *gymnasium*, too, where we made up around one-third of the student body. The other two-thirds were the local students who lived with their parents, and to some extent there were already a few genuine Nazis among them, which of course inevitably led to conflicts.

I can still remember well how in 1940 we drove to the castle in Tittmoning, which meanwhile had been converted into a country boarding school. A vehement confrontation developed when the Nazis sang songs mocking the Church. Then we seminarians joined forces and conducted a debate that might have led to violence if the teacher had not arrived just in time. Now he himself was a Nazi, too, but he wanted to give the appearance of neutrality, as though he were mediating between the two groups. But of course we were a thorn in the Nazis' side; we knew it and came to feel it on a regular basis.

After the passage of the "Hitler Youth Law" on December 1, 1936, it was a duty for all fourteen-year-olds to enter the Hitler Youth; with the enactment of the "second enforcement order" dated March 25, 1939, they could be compelled by the police to do so even against the will of the parents. From that point on, a distinction was made between the "core H.Y.", those who had previously entered voluntarily, and the "compulsory H.Y.", those who had been incorporated into it by force as a result of this law. Unlike the "core H.Y.", the "compulsory H.Y." members received no uniform, which identified them, so to speak, as second-class German youths. All girls had to join the "League of German Girls". In order to go through the formality at least of obeying this law and to avoid further sanctions that would have resulted from noncompliance, from then on the seminary registered all the boys who had reached that age with the H.Y. That was the case with Georg Ratzinger as well as with Joseph two years later.

As early as 1938, we were registered by the seminary with the Hitler Youth (HY) and then virtually by class assigned to various groups of the compulsory HY. That was the law, there were no exemptions, and furthermore the seminary would have run the risk of being shut down if it had not complied. That did not change until the beginning of the war, when the seminary was closed and turned into a military hospital. Consequently, all the minor seminarians became students at the public schools and lived with their parents or relatives again. With that, the compulsory HY collapsed; from then on it existed only on paper, because the seminarians had suddenly scattered to the four winds. We seminarians, naturally, no longer felt obliged to go to the meetings.

On August 9, 1938, the Bavarian Ministry of Education and Religious Affairs issued an order that henceforth the discount in tuition would be granted only to students, both boys and girls, who belonged to the HY. Although the monthly pension of the retired policeman Joseph Ratzinger at that time was only 242 reichsmark, he refused to get involved in it.

The boy next door to us, whose name was Albert, was an HY leader. The neighbor lady was always telling our mother that Georg (meaning me) and Joseph should go to Albert's HY meetings after all, and then they would have nothing to worry about. But our father did not want that, and of course we did not, either, although a tuition discount would have eased the family budget considerably. Then there was the mathematics teacher, who was temporarily the headmaster—as I mentioned, more or less a Nazi—and he, too, by all means wanted my brother to go to the HY meetings, because he would then get a tuition discount. In a way, it was actually well intentioned, I must say. But my brother told him quite clearly: "No, I will not do that." Then the teacher, for all his Nazi views, somehow understood and just said, "Okay, then we will leave it at that." So Joseph no longer had to go to the HY meetings.

In an interview with Peter Seewald, the future Pope Benedict XVI explained: "As soon as I was out of the seminary, I never went back. And that was difficult, because the tuition reduction, which I really needed, was tied to proof of attendance at the HY. Thank goodness, there was a very understanding mathematics teacher. He himself was a Nazi but an honest man, who said to me, 'Just go once and get the document so that we have it. . . .' When he saw that I simply didn't want to, he said, 'I understand, I'll take care of it', and so I was able to stay free of it" (SE 52). The British press campaign about "Ratzinger the Hitler Youth" was sheer nonsense, as proved also by elderly residents of Traunstein who were tracked down by the Frankfurter Allgemeine Zeitung *[a daily newspaper in Frankfurt]. Joseph Friedrich Schmitt, for example, although he attended the modern secondary school, knew Joseph Ratzinger from elementary school; he remembers "that it was possible for the seminarians in Traunstein to be exempted from the service". Generally the National Socialists were hostile toward candidates for the priesthood. Franz Mitterreiter, whose now-deceased brothers Alois and Ludwig attended the seminary together with the Ratzinger brothers, confirmed that they, too, did not have to go to HY functions more than once or twice. Besides, nobody would have wanted to have them around, because they were suspected of putting up resistance and undermining the faith of other Hitler Youths in the regime.*

While in the seminary, we also experienced the death of Pope Pius XI (*1922–1939*) and the election of Pius XII (*1939–1958*) as his successor. That was the first time in our life, for either me or Joseph, that a pontificate ended and a new one began, for Pius XI had been pope all through our childhood. I can still remember clearly how it was: early one Sunday morning a technically gifted prefect received on his private radio a rather long transmission from Rome about the new pope, which he then relayed to our study halls by means of the loudspeakers that were set up in them. Of course we were all very interested in this report and followed it quite attentively. Previously the rector of our seminary (*Johann Evangelist Mair*), who was a very venerable and intellectually distinguished priest, had told the local pastor by telephone that the Secretary of State, Cardinal Pacelli, would become the new pope. The local pastor could not or would not believe it, and so the two bet on it. Naturally our seminary rector won the bet, which increased our respect for him even more. He then explained to us that Pacelli was a very spiritual man of great intelligence and courage, which is why he welcomed his election. He probably knew him from the time when Pius XII, as he was now called, had been apostolic nuncio in Germany, first in Munich, then in Berlin. In any case, we had great respect for the new pope from the beginning and felt that he was the right man for the Petrine office.

In September 1939 the seminary was requisitioned as an immediate consequence of the outbreak of war, so that at first we again went to school from home. I do not know, however, whether the wounded were really being transported to Traunstein already. At any rate, the house was released again by the military a few months later, and we were allowed to return to the seminary for the time being. Yet a little later it was requisitioned for the second time, and we were evacuated, some of us to Sparz to a house of the English Sisters, but also to other larger houses. Thus some of us—it may have been twenty boys— found accommodations with the pastor in Waging, who had a large rectory he did not need, where a community of priests had once lived. At that time more and more ecclesiastical buildings were being confiscated by the Nazis. It started very quietly, but soon their intention became obvious.

In any case, Joseph and Georg Ratzinger lived in the English Sisters' former institute for girls. It was vacant now, because the Nazis had closed the convent schools. For Joseph, the new boarding school had one distinct advantage: there was no athletic field. Instead, the students hiked in the afternoon in the extensive woods in that area or played beside a nearby mountain stream. There they built dams and caught fish, which was altogether to his taste. So during this time, he was reconciled with the seminary and had to admit that the give and take in a community did him good.

Joseph then really began to cope well, because at the seminary he was able to make good friends with whom he liked to spend time together. Then everything was less upsetting, although boarding school life was naturally more difficult and demanding than life at home with parents.

The brothers tried, at least, to make the best of the circumstances in that historical period. In early 1938, Hitler's troops had marched into Austria, and, for the next seven years, the land on either side of the Danube belonged to the Reich. Although the borders had been closed after Hitler seized power, nothing stopped the brothers now from traveling to Salzburg. That led to a Mozart experience that left a lifelong impression on them both.

Actually we became acquainted with Mozart quite late. He didn't get to play a great part in our harmonium lessons or later in our piano lessons, because he did not compose for either of these instruments. Only when we attended the feast-day liturgies in Traunstein, at which Mozart Masses were also performed, did the name Mozart mean anything to us; of course, then we heard his works over the radio, too.

But our real encounter with Mozart took place when we were able to travel to Austria again, in other words, after the "annexation". We always liked to visit Salzburg. Together with our family, we used to travel up to Maria Plain to visit the miraculous image of "Mary, Comfort of the Afflicted", and we usually stayed until the prayer service in the evening. Maria Plain was important because Mozart first performed there his famous *Coronation* Mass on the occasion of the crowning of the miraculous image. We heard our first Mozart concert in 1939 or 1940, when the Munich Cathedral Choir performed the Mozart Requiem in the Mozarteum in Salzburg. At that time, it was directed by the house conductor, Meinhard von Zallinger (*1897–1990*), who later played a role in Munich. It fascinated us enormously.

In 1941, a Mozart Year was celebrated in Salzburg to commemorate the 150th anniversary of Mozart's death. At that time

I heard that the Regensburger Domspatzen were going to perform, who in those days were directed by Theobald Schrems.
Of course I did not want to miss that. Generally the Domspatzen sang little by Mozart, because his works as a rule are
accompanied by instruments, whereas the Domspatzen usually
sing a capella. At any rate I rode over there on my bicycle and
bought tickets for Joseph and me. When the time came, we two
cycled to Salzburg and stayed overnight at the Tiger Inn for
3.50 reichsmark, breakfast included. Today, prices like that are
unimaginable, but at the time it was a lot of money for us. That
is how we heard that wonderful concert by the Domspatzen. I
still know most of the program by heart today. The choir was
accompanied by several musicians from the Mozarteum and performed excerpts from Mozart's Requiem. Some boys sang the
"Bandel Trio", with simplified coloratura, of course, since there
are several really difficult passages in it. We were simply delighted
with it, the music was so wonderful. Naturally, at that point in
time there was no way I could have guessed that twenty-three
years later I would direct that same magnificent choir as cathedral choirmaster, but that is precisely how it would happen.

Another time we rode again to Salzburg to hear Mozart's C-minor
Mass in Saint Peter's Church; I think that today it is still performed on one Saturday during the music festival. For us, it was
like an excursion into an entirely new world that thrilled us and
cast its spell over us. This music was completely new territory for
us, because there were no concerts like that in Aschau or Traunstein. So for the first time in our lives, we had the privilege of attending a concert with top-quality interpretations of musical masterpieces
that meant a lot to us. It left a deep impression on us. So Mozart,
I think, is my brother's favorite composer even today. Of course
he likes other composers and their masterpieces, too, for instance
the wonderful Bach Passions, the B-minor Mass by Bach, and
Haydn, too, wrote very beautiful Masses. Still, I think that Mozart
appeals to him the most.

At around the same time, he began to take an interest in literature, also. In German class at the *gymnasium*, of course, the
great literary masterpieces of past centuries were read, which he
found very interesting. But besides this "required reading" for
school, he enthusiastically read other things that were not part
of the curriculum. He especially liked the little paperback reprints
of famous works published by Reclam; the thinner ones used to
cost 45 cents. One of his favorite authors at that time was Theodor Storm, but we all liked him a lot. He read, for instance,
Pole Poppenspäler (*Paul the Puppeteer*), *Der Schimmelreiter* (*The White
Horseman*), and many other fascinating works by Storm.[2] In addition, Joseph liked Eduard Mörike's *Mozart auf der Reise nach Prag*
(*Mozart on the Way to Prague*). He did not like Schiller very much;
he was a little too lofty for him. But he greatly esteemed Goethe.
To be honest, I found out only later that he himself tried his
hand at writing at that point in time.

*When Hitler celebrated his major triumphs in 1940, there was euphoria
almost everywhere. Only Joseph Ratzinger, Sr., stubbornly refused to
be swept up in it. A victory for Hitler, he explained, could never be a
victory for Germany. It was only a victory of the Antichrist, which
would necessarily bring about apocalyptic times for all believers and not
only for them. One year later, while young Joseph Ratzinger's class was
on a boat ride on a nearby lake, the invasion of the Soviet Union was
announced. It seemed as though a nightmare had come true. Now the
youth, too, was sure that Hitler would inevitably fail in the endless
expanses of Russia as Napoleon had once done.*

As far as our father was concerned, Hitler was the Antichrist,
even though perhaps he did not use the term directly, at least

---

[2] The North German author Theodor Storm (1817–1888) from Husum on the North
Sea made a name for himself as a poet and author of novellas and prose, developing a
North German, middle-class variety of German realism. Even today his last and best-
known work, *Der Schimmelreiter*, is a popular book on school reading lists.

not in my presence. And so the Führer's initial triumphs caused Father some embarrassment, because he had not counted on that. And it was as though his worst fears had come true: that first Poland was conquered in just a few weeks and then early the next year France, too, of which our father had such a high opinion—he simply could not believe it. After all, France had established the Maginot Line after the First World War; that was supposed to be a very clever and impregnable defense, and for that reason alone the French felt safe from the Germans. But Hitler, who had no scruples, went around it by invading peaceful, neutral Belgium. Therefore we could not help but be afraid that Hitler might win the war, which of course could not be and, so, was simply unthinkable.

The most vivid sign that we were at war was the fact that in the evening the windows had to be blacked out to protect against aerial attacks. There was an ordinance that no light was allowed to show outside. This was accomplished with black-out paper, which was fastened to each window with a small bar when evening came. The Nazis monitored compliance to make sure that indeed no light emerged from the house.

Then food ration cards were distributed. You could no longer buy groceries whenever you needed them. Instead, each registered person received food ration cards, with which he was allowed to purchase only the quantity allotted to him, so many grams of lard, so many grams of meat, sugar, or baked goods. Then you had to see how you could get by with that amount. Fortunately, Father was well acquainted with several farmers in the area around Traunstein. He often cycled to their farms and purchased additional food for us, so we always had enough to eat.

Meanwhile, the horrors of war moved closer and closer to the Salzach valley. With increasing frequency, transports with wounded servicemen from the front arrived in Traunstein, and a funeral service was held in the church for one of the fallen soldiers. Soon there were among them young men whom the Ratzinger brothers knew from the gymnasium. The military hospital had to be expanded, and finally all the seminarians again went back home. In the summer of 1942, Georg Ratzinger was first called up for the work service of the Reich.

In the work service, fortunately, they did not know we were seminarians; we were simply considered to be "workmen". Half of the team was made up of high school students and recent graduates from Upper Bavaria, and the other half, Slovenians. Only a few of the Slovanians spoke German at all. We were divided into sixteen troops, and to each troop was assigned one Slovenian who had some command of our language. Our deployment was in Wartenberg am Roll, which was located in the Sudetenland. Our first task was "with muscle power and spades" to lay out a sports field—of all things, a sports field!

One particular exercise was the daily drill with the spades, the so-called "spade roll-call". It was nothing short of a liturgy, a military exercise with an implement that was actually quite insignificant. Moreover, the spade had to be clean and polished; you had to be able to see your reflection in it, for if even a speck of dust or a clump of earth was left on the shovel or the handle, it was considered a serious offense that was punished with remedial exercises. Then the commands resounded over the field: "Attention! Invert spades! Lift spades! Shoulder spades! Port spades! Present spades! Order spades!" It was like a drill with weapons in the military. Everything had to take place precisely in tempo, simultaneously, as it were, so that the whole team looked as though one man were doing it all with that clean, polished spade. In order to make the exercises of this spade-worship look good, we were specially trained for them. Of course we had to perform the whole thing again and again whenever our division was visited, for it was a well-staged show, in which one or two hundred men shouldered their spades and put them down again in synchronized maneuvers, however idiotic and useless it all was.

Deployment in the Sudetenland, however, was only the sad prelude to deployment in the war. Scarcely had I returned to Traunstein in November 1942 when I was drafted into the Wehrmacht after two weeks of leave. A bleak mood prevailed in our family. I was sad that I had to go away from home again, and my family was unhappy that I was going into the military. We all knew that that was a bad thing, that men in the service were ill-treated, but above all that I now had to serve a government we despised with all our hearts. First I was sent to Oberammergau, of which I had already heard because of the famous Passion play. There at least my father and my brother were able to visit me, and it was there that I had to shoot for the first time. Ironically, I was the best shot then, which gained for me a certain prestige. Actually, as it later appeared, I was a mediocre shot, but in those first attempts I was just fortunate.

Then we were sent to Holland. There each one of us received a bicycle, and every day we had to ride out into the dunes to drill there. We wore boots that were full of sand afterward. Once I had to participate also in a horse transport, since my company had a lot of horses. It was, so to speak, a punitive expedition. At that time we always had to clean our weapons until they gleamed, and they checked this thoroughly: the tiniest grain of sand could not be left. I was with the machine gun division then, and one day, on the day before the Ascension of our Lord in 1943, our commanding officer was not satisfied with my cleaning skills. And so I, along with the others whose machine guns were not entirely clean, was sent off to a cavalry detachment. Early in the morning on the feast of the Ascension, we had to travel by train from Leiden to Alphen. There they brought us to a gigantic hall that served as a stable. Our *Capo*, our noncommissioned officer, then chose a few horses for us, and each one, myself included, had the reins of two horses pressed into his hand. I had a sickening feeling, because shortly before that a neighbor's son, who was one of my best friends, had been kicked by a horse and lost his life, and so I did not want to die that way.

There were around thirty-five of us men, who were supposed to lead seventy horses, and we were told to march out, one after the other. My horses probably noticed quickly that they did not have an energetic leader, and they took advantage of the opportunity: again and again they tried to leave the street and go into the field, where fresh clover beckoned. When the noncommissioned officer noticed it, he vehemently reprimanded me. Shortly thereafter, he himself got kicked by a horse, which seemed to me not all that unjust. Finally we drew near to the city of Leiden. Apparently my horses got wind of the city air and were longing for a stall. At any rate, they began to run and overtook the other horses, while I ran behind them, and so we reached the barracks first, although to begin with we had been the last. Naturally that caused some laughter among my comrades.

Then our unit was transferred to Italy, at first in the East, on the Ligurian Coast near La Spezia, and later to the vicinity of Monte Cassino, the site of the world-renowned Benedictine monastery. The Germans had set up their line of defense there and were exposed to constant, massive bombardments by the Americans and the British.

On February 15, 1944, the Allies had bombed even the monastery on Monte Cassino, which had been established in A.D. 529, because they suspected a German emplacement behind its walls. That was a disastrous mistake, as it later turned out; the commander in chief of the German troops, General Field Marshall Albert Kesselring, had expressly declined to misuse this unique cultural monument for military purposes. In the bombardment, 250 people lost their lives, most of them monks and refugees who had sought refuge behind the monastery walls.

We reached the area around Cassino when the monastery was already lying in ruins. The Americans had established their bridgehead near Nettuno in order to bypass the main German line of defense so as to be able to advance more quickly to Rome. So in our position, we were exposed to constant fire from two sides. It was like being in hell down there; it was always thundering, God knows how. Once they told us that we all had to get out of our positions, the Americans were about to attack. We were lying on the ground at a distance of four or five yards from each other when I noticed my neighbor was no longer moving. That was when I saw that his whole hip was bloody and that he was already dead. Then we had to stand up and begin our retreat. Each one had his weapon, his ammunition pouch, and all his gear. The Americans followed us with tanks; we were moving on foot. Then we marched to Rome. In view of Saint Peter's Basilica, we were allowed to come to a halt. We were dead tired. Despite that, I would have been so glad to go into that magnificent church just for a prayer, but it was forbidden. Churches in general were off limits to us. Then came the command: Continue the march, and leave the city by a particular street, the Via Cassia. We also heard the shouts of joy of the populace as we left Rome. The people were glad when the Americans arrived and we were gone, and who could blame them.

My brother told me how Professor Hubert Jedin (1900–1980), the famous Church historian, experienced the events of that time. His mother was of Jewish extraction, and so he had fled to the Vatican, which he was not allowed to leave during the nine months of the German occupation. He had observed how the Germans pulled back from Rome on foot and the American army moved in with their trucks. The Germans made such a weary, downtrodden impression that people could already tell how it all would end, that they had already lost the war.

By the Via Cassia we reached Bolsena, a little town in Latium, north of Rome, where a famous eucharistic miracle took place during the Middle Ages.

A Bohemian priest on a pilgrimage to Rome in 1263 was offering the Sacrifice of the Mass in the Church of Saint Christina when doubts occurred to him about the presence of the Lord in the Eucharist, in other words, about the transubstantiation of bread and wine into the Body and Blood of Christ. But at the moment when he broke the Host, blood dripped from it, human blood, onto the altar cloth. The miracle was reported immediately to the pope, who was staying at the time in Orvieto, and the altar cloth with the large bloodstain was brought there. Today it is still displayed in the cathedral in Orvieto. Subsequently the pope reigning then, Urban IV (1261–1264), inaugurated the Feast of Corpus Christi.

There, in Bolsena, on June 12, 1944, we engaged the Americans in a firefight and tried to stop them. During the battle, a grenade exploded near me, and the force swept up my arms—and then I saw that my right upper arm was bleeding heavily. I drew my arm back right away and thanked God that I could still move it. Nevertheless, I was afraid I might never be able to play music again, and for me that was a rather depressing thought. In any case, I crawled to the nearest Red Cross tank, torturously made my way into it with difficulty and a lot of pain, and let them bring me to a cave where the Red Cross treated the wounded. An assistant doctor was there, who first cut open my sleeve and treated me. The whole arm was so completely covered with dried blood that initially he could not find the wound. But then he discovered the point of entry on the one side and the exit wound on the other. Apparently at the moment when my arms went up, an enemy bullet had gone clear through my arm. "That's a nice million-dollar wound", was his mildly ironic comment on the gunshot wound, which was actually quite harmless, and he was right. After making several stops, an ambulance brought me to Rosenheim, where there was an assembly point for the sick. There I saw how much suffering the war had inflicted on the young men of my generation, many of whom were now crippled because they had to have a leg or an arm amputated. Fortunately, there was a very reasonable senior medical officer there.

He himself had once been wounded and brought to a military hospital, in which he had felt very lonely, and so he had resolved to grant each soldier his wish. Therefore he asked me where I wanted to go, and naturally I answered, "To Traunstein." So I was transferred as a wounded soldier to the military hospital in Traunstein, on the premises of our former seminary. Around that time, specifically on July 20, 1944, the attempt to assassinate Hitler took place, but we heard little about it in the military hospital. Of course we would have hoped the war would end right then, but, as everyone knows, that was unfortunately not the case. Yet at least I could recuperate from the hardships of war in Traunstein. Soon I had full use of my arm again, too, which was a big relief for me. The nurses gave me good food, the usual ration and always a little more besides. Every ten days, I got a new medical chart, on which my present weight was also noted, and after ten days it said that I had already gained twenty-two pounds. At first I had no doubt about that, but then it turned out the scale was broken. At any rate, I spent a few nice days there in my former seminary during which I quickly regained my strength. So I was soon assigned to a convalescent company and was sent first to Prague and then to the Czech hinterland. There we had to fell trees and cut them up into small pieces. We used to say we were only making cheap firewood for the Czechs, and that was precisely the case. When our convalescent company was stationed in a little town, they told us at first that we would be transferred to Yugoslavia to serve as a guerilla unit. But the assistant officer of our division prevented that and managed to have us transferred to Italy to rejoin our troop. At that time, I came to the region around Imola and was assigned to the radio unit. That meant in practice that during the day I stayed in the bunker and at night had to go out to repair broken telephone lines, which was a rather dangerous job.

Our next position, near Dozza in the province of Bologna, was hell on earth. We were situated on the north side of Monte

Maggiore, while the Americans opened fire on us from the south side. Actually they shot at the cliffs over us, and again and again fragments of rock broke off from them and fell down on us. Then there was dust and a roar, and as soon as there was a pause in the fire, we first had to fortify our bunkers. One day, on April 15, 1945, the artillery fire suddenly stopped, and they began launching white phosphorus shells that turned the mountain slope into a sea of flames. Everything around us was burning, all the bushes and trees. The next day began with a deathly silence that was almost ghostly. For a moment we thought the war was over. But then the Americans stormed our bunker with fixed bayonets and a shout that set our teeth on edge and drove us out. First, they took our watches and then our medals. I had two decorations, one for being wounded in action and then the Iron Cross Second Class, which was awarded to everyone who had mended the broken telephone lines a few times. In a roundabout way, they brought us to a prison camp near Vesuvius, where there were several camps, each for four thousand captured soldiers. At first we were guarded by white soldiers, but then they were relieved by black Americans, who took everything a little easier. It even happened occasionally that they fell asleep at their guard posts and their weapons fell down—to us in the camp. That was of course a serious offense for which they were usually disciplined. So we used to snap up the weapon and sell it back to the guard for cigarettes. It was not long before the colored soldiers were replaced by Italians. We welcomed them by stacking our tin cans in such a way that they looked like canon barrels, which we then aimed at them. So the Italians thought we were in possession of heavy artillery, and they fled immediately, so that for a time we were on our own again.

Finally the American administration organized a train that would transport the first group of prisoners to be released. They had instructed some German soldiers whom they trusted to some degree, including theologians, to draw up the necessary list of

persons. The first plan was to give preference to all vitally important occupations, in other words, farm workers, transportation
workers, in short, all the workers. But shortly thereafter, this
order was revoked, and they said that everyone from the eastern
part of Germany had to remain in the camp. Therefore, the first
train of released prisoners was reorganized, and one of the theologians who knew me put me on this list. So I returned home
by the first train of released prisoners that traveled from Italy to
Germany. That was in mid-July of 1945.

*Joseph Ratzinger did not escape the war, either. In 1943 the brown-
shirted rulers had a new idea. Since boarding-school students lived in
community away from home anyway, they reasoned, you could relocate
their boarding schools arbitrarily—for instance, to the batteries of the
Flugabwehr (anti-aircraft defense, or "Flak"). Since they could not spend
the whole day studying, it would make sense for them to spend their
free time defending against enemy planes. Thus, the seminarians from
Traunstein who were born in 1926 and 1927 were drafted into the Flak
and went to Munich. They lived in barracks like the regular soldiers,
wore similar uniforms, and had almost the same duties. The only difference was that in addition they took a reduced load of courses taught
by the teachers from the Maximilians-Gymnasium in Munich. Since
the students of that school had likewise been drafted, it was a mixed
class. For Joseph, it was an exciting experience suddenly to meet with
students of the same age from the big city. After some initial friction,
everyone learned to get along and to form a community.*

*Their first post was Ludwigsfeld to the north of Munich. Their duty
there was to protect a branch of the Bavarian Motor Works (BMW)
that manufactured airplane motors. Later they were transferred to Unter-
föhring, then to Innsbruck, and finally to Gilching, to the west of Munich,
where the Dornier-Werke were located. Since the Allied bombers gathered in that same airspace for their attacks on Munich, the position was
doubly important. For the sixteen-year-old Joseph Ratzinger, who once
described himself as being "so nonmilitary a person" (M 31), it was a*

Flak assistant Joseph Ratzinger, second from the left, 1943

difficult time. Nevertheless, he tried to make the best of it. He asked to be assigned to the observation division and then to telephone communications and thus could at least avoid having to shoot. He was fortunate: the noncommissioned officer in charge of them relentlessly defended the autonomy of his group. At some point or other, the group was exempted from all military exercises, and no one dared to intrude into their little world. Finally, he was even assigned to a little single room in one of the barracks. He used every spare minute to read and, with a large group of active Catholics in the unit, was able to organize, first, religious instruction and, then, occasional visits to churches. One of the men who served in the same Flak battery with him, the now eighty-four-year-old Walter Fried of Munich, still remembers well the "very reserved, relatively unpretentious" youth. Once, he related to the news magazine Der Spiegel, *a high-ranking officer came by for an inspection. Then, one after the other, each had to say what he wanted to be someday. Many, including Fried, said they wanted to become a pilot. In that case, there were no further questions. "When Ratzinger's turn came, he said he wanted to become a priest. There was some derisive laughter. But of course at that time it did take some courage to give such an answer."*

At first, the students were still allowed to go into the city three times a week to attend classes at the Maximilians-Gymnasium. But gradually the trips turned into a nightmare. The city was bombarded with increasing frequency by the Allies, and it seemed to be sinking more and more into ruins. Soon there was nothing in the air but smoke and an intense smell of fire. Finally, rail travel was no longer possible; a bomb attack had destroyed the tracks. The seminarians hoped that the Western powers would succeed and end the war as soon as possible. Yet several of them would not live to see the end of the war.

On September 10, 1944, the students were released from the Flak. Yet no sooner had Joseph arrived in Traunstein than he received his draft notice to report to the work service of the Reich. After an endless ride on a truck bed, his battalion arrived in the Austrian Burgenland. There an enormous army of forced laborers was supposed to erect a "southeastern rampart" post-haste, in order to stop the advance of the Russians. The next two months were the most horrible time of his life, for the SS officers were in command. The young men endured nothing short of enslavement. In the night, they were summoned from their plank beds in the barracks and pressured to enlist "voluntarily" in the weapons branch of the SS. Many who were too exhausted to offer resistance became obliged in this way to serve the monster. When Ratzinger said he had the intention of becoming a Catholic priest, he was ridiculed and insulted. But at least that chalice passed from him.

In the Reich work service, the seventeen-year-old realized for the first time the pseudo-religious character of National Socialism, "Hitler's religion" in pure form. Like his brother, Georg, he too was "trained according to a ritual invented in the 1930s, which was adapted from a kind of 'cult of the spade', that is, a cult of work as redemptive power", as he wrote in his memoirs, Milestones (33). Picking up and putting down the spade, cleaning it, and presenting it seemed to him like a "pseudo-liturgy". Only when the front drew closer did the spade rituals come to an abrupt end. Suddenly the spade was once again what it really always had been: a banal, everyday tool. Its "fall", however, was emblematic of the collapse of National Socialism that was now unmistakably occurring everywhere: "A full-scale liturgy and the world behind it were being unmasked as a lie" (M 34).

Usually work service personnel at the front were automatically taken over by the armed forces. Yet Joseph Ratzinger was again lucky. First, he was sent back home, completely unexpectedly. He started his journey by taking the train, which had to stop again and again when air-raid alarms sounded. The trip led through Vienna, which now also bore the scars of bombardment during the war. In his beloved Salzburg, not only was the train station in ruins, but the beautiful Renaissance cathedral also appeared to have been hit. As the train was about to travel right through Traunstein because of an aerial threat, he quickly decided to jump off.

Finally he was at home. "It was an idyllically beautiful fall day", he later recalled: "There was a bit of hoarfrost on the trees, and the mountains glowed in the afternoon sun. Seldom have I ever experienced the beauty of my homeland as on this return from a world disfigured by ideology and hatred" (M 34). He never liked the military. Now, however, after he had experienced first hand the horrors of war, he first realized how precious peace was.

But the war was not yet over. After a "welcome respite" of three weeks, he was called to Munich. There the officer who had to assign the young men probably no longer believed in "final victory", either. "What shall we do with you? Where is your home?" he asked the young man. "In Traunstein", Joseph answered. "We have a barracks there," the officer replied, "so go to Traunstein, and don't start right away, but enjoy a few nice days first" (see M 35).

So first he had to go through basic training in the barracks in Traunstein. In a dejected mood, he celebrated a melancholy Christmas in 1944 with his comrades in their living quarters. When he became sick, he was exempt from service for almost the entire month of February. In general, the chief duty of his company seemed to be marching through the city in new uniforms and singing war songs to prove to the public that the "Führer" still had young, freshly trained soldiers at his disposal. Then, when there was still a danger of being called to the front, Joseph took courage—and simply deserted.

At that time—this was in April 1945—he was risking his life, because the SS had orders to shoot deserters on the spot or to hang them on the nearest tree as a warning to anyone who might try to imitate them. When two soldiers confronted him at a railroad underpass, his heart sank. But he was lucky again. Obviously the two armed servicemen were just as sick and tired of the war as he was. And since he had his arm in a sling because of an injury, they let him pass. "Comrade, you are wounded. Move on!" So, finally, he arrived home unharmed.

But even there he was not safe. A few days later, two SS men were quartered in his parents' house. They saw the young man of military age and began to ask uncomfortable questions. When his father then aired his angry opinions about Hitler, it seemed that his fate was sealed. But for inscrutable reasons, the two Nazis disappeared again the next day without having caused any mischief.

Finally, the Americans marched into Traunstein. Even though it was so modest, they made the Ratzinger house their headquarters. When they identified Joseph as a former soldier, he had to put on his uniform and surrender formally. His mother was horrified when she learned that her son was now considered a prisoner of war. She quickly prepared for him some semolina gruel, while he himself put an empty notebook and a pencil in his pocket before setting out together with several hundred other prisoners of war from his small town on the path to an uncertain future.

It was an almost endless parade, which after a three-day march on the empty highway finally arrived at Bad Aibling. The Allies had gathered the survivors of the defeated army from all parts of Bavaria and rounded them up there on a former military airfield. Especially the very young and the very old soldiers were enthusiastically photographed again and again. The Americans wanted to show back home the desperate straits in which the Germans had already been. From Bad Aibling, the men were finally transported to an immense tract of farmland near Ulm, on which the approximately 50,000 prisoners were accommodated. Since the Americans were completely overwhelmed by the magnitude of these numbers, there were neither barracks nor tents; the men had to spend the night in the open. A lucky few had brought their own tents along

and offered their comrades shelter when it rained. The daily rations con-
sisted of a ladle of soup and a bit of bread. On the horizon loomed the
tower of the cathedral in Ulm, which had not been damaged during the
war, as a sign of hope for a better time and a reminder of the indomi-
table humaneness of the faith.

The prisoners lived without any sense of time; only with difficulty
could they figure out exactly what day it was, and they received no news
at all from outside. On one occasion, though, the men noticed that the
Americans set off some real fireworks with their pyrotechnic rounds. It
was May 8, 1945. At one point, the rumor circulated that the war was
over; Germany had capitulated. The men breathed more easily and
hoped that consequently their release was imminent. Then someone main-
tained that the Americans were now going to advance against the Rus-
sians. Supposedly they intended to arm all the German POWs and
send them into the new war. But most of them could not imagine that
the league of the Allies would break up so quickly, and they hoped for
peace soon. The notebook that Joseph Ratzinger had brought with him
into imprisonment proved to be wonderful company. Every day he entrusted
to it his thoughts and reflections about God and the world, history, and
his situation. He even tried his hand at a few Greek hexameters so as
to keep his mind occupied and to fill the empty time. In the camp, too,
initiatives were soon taken by men who tried to derive something useful
from the desolate incarceration. Priests were found who celebrated Holy
Mass each day, and academics developed a real lecture series.

Then the releases began. At first farmers were allowed to go home, and,
understandably enough, very many suddenly remembered they had a farm
or at least relatives in the country. Finally, on June 19, 1945, Joseph Rat-
zinger had his turn, too. After a series of reviews and examinations, and
after being sprayed with insecticides—somehow the Americans thought all
Germans had lice—he finally held his release certificate in his hands. A
U.S. truck brought a group of men as far as northern Munich, and from
there on they had to fend for themselves. Joseph and a young man from a
neighboring village set out on the road. They had calculated that it would
take them three days to travel the approximately 75 miles to Traunstein.

They hoped that along the way they could spend the night at farmhouses and perhaps get something to eat there. But they had just passed Ottobrunn when a milk truck running on wood gas overtook them. The two young men were too shy to flag it down, and so the driver himself stopped and asked where they were headed. When they mentioned Traunstein, he laughed; he belonged to a dairy in Traunstein and was making the trip back. Even before sunset, Joseph was home. Overjoyed, his parents and his sister welcomed him. The simple meal his mother quickly prepared for him—a small salad from the garden, an egg from the chickens, and a big piece of bread—became the most delicious meal of his life. Only one thing troubled the joy of their reunion: it was still uncertain what had become of his brother. Only later in July did a tanned Georg suddenly stand in front of the house, too . . .

We, too, were brought at first from Italy to the big release camp near Bad Aibling, where my brother had been only a few weeks before. Later Günter Grass told about meeting him there, but he probably just imagined the incident. Maybe he really was at that camp, but in another place or at another point in time. My brother has such an excellent memory that he surely would be able to remember it even today if he had dug a hole, played dice, and spoken about his future with a fellow prisoner who wanted to become an artist. That may be a nice story, but it is not a true one.

In 2006, Günter Grass, a winner of the Nobel Prize for Literature, claimed in his autobiography, Beim Häuten der Zwiebel [Peeling the Onion], that he was with Joseph Ratzinger in the prisoner of war camp near Bad Aibling and at that time befriended the future pope. Later, in an interview with Frank Schirrmacher, the publisher of the Frankfurter Allgemeine Zeitung, Grass said: "I always sat in the camp in Bad Aibling together with guys my own age. We seventeen-year-olds used to squat, when it rained, in a hole we had dug for ourselves. We had spread a tarp over it to keep out the rain. One hundred thousand prisoners of war were gathered there in the open.

And one of them was named Joseph, who was extremely Catholic and occasionally uttered quotations in Latin. He became my friend and dice partner, for I had been able to salvage a dice-box and bring it to the camp. We spent time together, played dice, talked, and speculated about the future, as youngsters like to do. I wanted to become an artist, and he wanted to have a career in the Church. He seemed a bit stuck-up to me, but he was a nice fellow. That really is a nice story, don't you think?"

In any case, I arrived there a few weeks later and found an immense crowd of soldiers who had to camp there under the most miserable circumstances. There was practically no blanket, no tent, nothing. We were fed a brown soup, a cup of coffee, and a few pieces of bread. At night you went to sleep simply by lying on the bare ground; thank heavens we had nice weather and were released after only three days.

On that third day, an American officer came into the camp, and we all had to stand in formation. Then he arranged us in groups geographically: *Oberbayern* (Upper Bavaria), *Unterbayern*—he actually said *"Unterbayern"* and apparently did not know that the correct term is *"Niederbayern"* (Lower Bavaria)—and so on. He handed our regional group over to a black American, who brought us to a group of trucks that were all driven by colored soldiers. There he assigned me to the group of men who wanted to go to Traunstein. A later priest confrere, who was ordained after me, was there, too. No sooner had we boarded the truck than the black driver started off at a hellish speed; first he drove along the Munich-Salzburg highway and finally took the exit at Schweinbach, while chewing his gum the entire time, which for us was a rather unusual sight. Then he stopped and shouted something to us, and we got off feeling rather sick to our stomachs. Furthermore, I did not know whether my parents and my brother were still alive or whether our house still stood, for it was months since I had been in touch with anyone back home. Nevertheless, I ran rather than walked to my parents' house.

The last photo of the family residence in Hufschlag near Traunstein before their move (1955) shows Georg Ratzinger (right) and his parents

When I was finally home, I saw Mother outside pumping water; we had our own well in front of the house, because water mains had not yet been laid. I was so happy to see her again, and it was a big surprise and a joy for her, too. I had waited so long for that moment! After we had embraced, we went into the house, where my father and my siblings were actually waiting only for Mother. What happened then cannot be described in words; you simply had to be there. Even before I said anything, I sat right down at the piano and played the *Te Deum*: "Holy God, we praise Thy Name." To me it was no coincidence that we could all be together again but, rather, a providential arrangement; we all were of the same opinion at the time. The fact that we had come through so many trying situations during the war unscathed confirmed us both, my brother

The young priests with their family in July 1951

and me, in our conviction that God had plans for us. The experience of the war years, indeed, confronted us with feelings of fear we had not known before. We were forced into a world that had previously been completely unknown to us and that we would never have imagined to be so brutal. We literally looked death in the face. That brought with it a certain new orientation and caused us suddenly to treasure many things we had previously taken for granted. Yet it confirmed us all the more in our intention to try to become priests.

VI

Freising and Fürstenried

(1946–1951)

The period immediately after the war was a happy time for us. The fact that they were also difficult, meager years seemed to us a secondary matter. We had survived the war, but, above all, the godless regime that brought so much suffering upon the people had been conquered.

Now our father had always known that this would be the outcome. From the first day on, he saw that the war was lost, that Hitler had to lose it, because evil simply could not and must not be victorious. If Germany had won that war, it would not have been a gain for our country but, rather, a catastrophe for the whole world. Then Hitler, with his boundless egotism, would have ruled the world; then by his arbitrary will he would not have shaped it but rather deformed and terrorized it. For that reason alone, it was unthinkable to us that God, who is Lord of history, would allow his victory. Of course in the first years, there were several upsetting events, like the victories in Poland and France, but no sooner had he marched into the Soviet Union than what had to happen happened, and the path of destiny led the German Reich directly into a catastrophe.

Nevertheless, many things we learned after the war surpassed even our bleakest suspicions. Of course we knew already during the Nazi period that there were concentration camps in which people were murdered. After all, the Dachau concentration camp was located quite near Munich and was something about which we all had heard. From various acquaintances we learned that relatives of theirs had been put to death. That even touched our family. I remember, for instance, our cousin, the son of one of our mother's sisters, a very sweet, happy boy. He was mentally handicapped, though. So he was not capable of speaking correctly or of taking part in a conversation. I do not know what diagnosis was made of his condition; I myself was still in primary school at the time. Later we learned that the Nazis went to his house, took him away, and then murdered him, because in their inhuman ideology he was considered a "life not worth living". In Aschau we were acquainted with an old, childless married couple who were always so happy when we came to visit. One day the husband died of pneumonia, and the wife, Frau Westenthanner, had a gradual onset of dementia. We heard only that she was brought to Linz by government officials and died there. It was general knowledge that in the vicinity of Linz the Nazis gathered people who were mentally ill (or thought to be such) and, to their way of thinking, no longer useful to society, and then killed them. In those days, you said someone had been "gelinzt". The inhabitants of Linz did not know this expression, but among us it was a set phrase, and everybody knew what it meant when someone said that a person had been "gelinzt". Killing human beings who were useless, in the Nazis' opinion, or who just had a different world view was part of the Nazi agenda. Of course, all that was murder. Only after the war did we learn about the major genocide inflicted on the Jews, but even that horrible fact did not surprise us, because we knew that the Nazis were capable of any crime, that they feared nothing and thought and behaved in a really demonic way. The mass murder of the Jews was the summit, so to speak, the gruesome crowning achievement among their crimes and the ultimate proof of what unscrupulous, inhumane, and despicable criminals they were. It was different from their other murders, though, in the first place, because of the number of victims and the systematic way in which they were destroyed. In any case, we were profoundly shaken when we learned about it, but the murders of people whom we knew had already disillusioned us. Unfortunately we also knew that resistance from within could never have swept those criminals away; it had to happen from outside. Consequently, we regarded our so-called "enemies", Germany's military opponents, as our liberators, to whom we were grateful for having ended the Nazi reign of terror.

Anti-Semitism was never an issue either in my family or among our acquaintances. We regarded everyone as a fellow human being, even if he was a Nazi, although we were cautious about the Nazis from the start and kept our distance because we could not trust them. Yet neither in Aschau nor in Traunstein were we acquainted with any Jews, and so we did not hear much about the anti-Semitic outrages of 1933, Kristallnacht in 1938, or of course the deportation of Jews. Only in school, in the course on "National Socialist ideology" (NG) that was always taught on Saturday, did they try to persuade us that Jews were wicked. Then suddenly we were warned about the Jews in history class, too. Naturally, we never took that seriously, for we could tell where this claim originated and knew with what sort of lies and calumnies the Nazis worked. But neither did we ever have a personal encounter with a Jew; it was simply that not that many of them lived in East Bavarian villages and towns, and so it was not something we discussed.

Benedict XVI has made more intensive efforts at reconciliation with the Jews than any pope before him; this is evident from the mere fact that he has visited more synagogues than any of his predecessors—namely, the synagogue in Cologne in August 2005, a synagogue in New York in April 2008, and in January 2010 the synagogue in Rome. In Auschwitz and at the Holocaust Memorial Yad Vashem, he clearly denounced any form of anti-Semitism or anti-Jewish sentiment, and in Jerusalem he prayed at the Wailing Wall. Immediately after his installation, he wrote to the Jewish community of Rome, and he was the first pope to invite a rabbi to address the Synod of Bishops.

In his important two-volume study Jesus of Nazareth, *he not only cites Jewish commentators on the New Testament but also makes an effort to understand Jesus and his gospel in its original Jewish context. Instead of "older brothers", he describes the Jews as our "fathers in faith". Thus, he declared in an interview with Peter Seewald: "I must say that from the very first day when I began to study theology, the intrinsic unity of the Old and the New Covenants, of the two parts of Holy Scripture, was somehow immediately clear to me.... Then as Germans we were of course shaken by what had happened in the Third Reich, which gave us a special reason to look with humility and shame, and with love, upon the People of Israel" (LW 81–82).*

Naturally, as pope and as especially as a German, my brother knows the obligation he has to promote reconciliation with the Jews. On the one hand, this is a direct consequence of German history, but much of it also goes back to his intensive contacts with the Integrierte Gemeinde in Munich. I think that in grappling with the studies by Professor Ludwig Weimar and Professor Rudolf Pesch some things became clear to him about the importance of the dialogue with Judaism.

After a prehistory of over twenty years, the Katholische Integrierte Gemeinde (KIG, Catholic Integrated Community) was lifted from the baptismal font in 1968 by a group of Catholics in Munich. Their starting point had been questions that were raised after World War II: "What is wrong with our Church when, despite the many millions of baptized persons in Europe, Christians waged two world wars against each other in the twentieth century; when in spite of so many Christians, the social question broached over a hundred years ago could not be solved, so that death-dealing dictatorships and ideologies such as Communism and National Socialism were able to develop and dominate? What has gone missing from our Church, that her faithful could not prevent the Shoah, the murder of six million Jews during the Third Reich?" Consequently, the KIG is especially committed to understanding the New

Testament from a Jewish perspective and demands "that the Israel of the Old Testament be perceived anew in its significance as the root of the Church and that living Judaism be regarded as a correcting partner who reminds us of this root." Already as a theologian, Joseph Ratzinger had come into contact with the Integrierte Gemeinde; as Archbishop of Munich, he was to approve their statutes and recognize them as an independent "apostolic community" subject to the ecclesial supervision of the local ordinary.

Today I live in the immediate neighborhood of the Jewish community of Regensburg, which has its synagogue here on the same street, Luzengasse. Until recently it was under the direction of Herr Hans Rosengold (*1923–2011*), with whom I have always maintained a good, neighborly relationship. Sometimes he visited me, sometimes I him, as neighbors do, for he was really a very nice man whom I esteemed very highly. The caretaker of the community, a Jew who emigrated from Russia, is very friendly, too; he is extremely courteous and helpful. He knows that my vision is poor, and when something along the street is being repaired and there are obstacles, he comes out and guides me past it. He has often helped my housekeeper, too, Frau Heindl, and carried the heavy bag when she was coming home from shopping. He also stops by our house from time to time, brings us newspapers and Jewish matzos (unleavened wafers) and that sweet Pesach wine. Not long ago when I was in the hospital, because I had a knee operation, he even visited me there and brought me some grapes. He and his wife are just very dear, friendly people who can be an example of humaneness to everybody. When my brother was in Regensburg in 2006, the Jewish community provided kosher food for part of his entourage, his so-called *seguito.* So we really have a wonderful neighborly relationship. In the postwar years, we could never have even dreamed that relations between Germans and Jews would one day be so happily normalized as is the case nowadays. Naturally we are glad about that, and we are grateful for it.

But back to the events of 1945! During the years when I was away at war, Joseph became a man. When I was drafted in 1942, he was just sixteen years old and actually still just a kid; his voice had not fully changed, and he was somewhere between a boy and a man. When we saw each other again after the war, he was already completely grown up. Of course we had a lot to tell each other; I talked about my experiences in the war, and he about his. But when I was in the minor seminary, our paths had already diverged, and we were no longer together as much as in our care-free childhood. I also had different friends from his; more the boys who were interested in music, whereas my brother mainly had friends who were science-oriented. During our school years at the seminary, we were both so tied up by the daily schedule that we hardly had any time left to see each other, but of course we made up for it during vacations. But now, after the end of the war, we were living together again and were to spend at least the next few years more or less together again.

Shortly after the end of the war, on November 9th, 1945, our parents celebrated their 25th wedding anniversary. It was a time of great poverty, and so the celebration of this nonetheless beautiful jubilee was modest. The day began with Mass in the parish church, with my brother the celebrant. I played the organ and sang some hymns, while our sister sat in the pews with our parents. A few dear friends brought us small gifts, a jar of honey, for example. Then our mother, always so resourceful, made the most of the little we had and prepared a wonderful midday meal. It was the only wedding anniversary our parents were able to celebrate festively together. Our father had died a year before their 40th anniversary.

After the war, we appreciated even more the fact that we had a home with good, concerned parents and dear siblings. I must admit that I was always a bit sorry whenever I heard, for instance among the Domspatzen, that a boy was an only child. I have always been grateful to the good Lord that he set me on my path through life with siblings and that I was born into an intact family. Naturally, there was also occasional irritation about this or that, once in a while there was a difference of opinion, but most of the time peace prevailed in our house. The fact that I had a home where I knew I belonged is something for which I will thank the dear Lord for the rest of my life.

At that time we had to make sure first of all that we got hold of identification papers, because only someone with identification had a right to ration cards. Again, as during the war, the economy was run on a quota basis, so that each person was entitled to only a predetermined quantity of meat, sausage, butter, sugar, and so on, per month. In our case, besides identification papers, we also had to present our discharge papers from the American prisoner of war camp.

Soon it was said that all the men released from captivity had to show proof of employment. Then we turned first to our seminary and petitioned the rector, Johann Evangelist Mair, whom we had always respected highly. He did not want us to work somewhere else and allowed us to work in the seminary. So we did not have to go someplace where we were strangers and do jobs for which we were not at all qualified but, rather, had the privilege of staying where we liked.

In fact, our seminary desperately needed an overhaul. It was now completely empty, after having served during the war, first, as a military hospital and, just recently, through the UNRRA (United Nations Relief and Rehabilitation Administration), as temporary housing for refugees from East Germany and Rumania. So my brother and I rode each day by bicycle to the seminary and helped to reorganize it. There we even got something extra to eat from the canteen kitchen, without having to use our ration stamps. There were other ex-seminarians there who were happy just to meet again with old schoolmates.

Our main task was to carry tables, desks, and other pieces of furniture into the seminary building. In doing so, we also refurbished the office of one of the prefects. That was a lot of fun for all of us, because we knew we were doing something meaningful and were making our small contribution to the reconstruction. In the evening, we rode back home and there enjoyed the peace and quiet of our parents' house. So it continued well into the autumn.

On Saint Corbinian's day, November 20, 1945, all the seminarians who were home again met at the seminary for a great Solemn Mass of Thanksgiving. Saint Corbinian is the patron of the Archdiocese of Munich and Freising, the herald of the faith who came to us more than 1,200 years ago from France. This reunion on his feast day was very uplifting and joyful for us.

Saint Corbinian is still today one of the most revered saints in Bavaria. His relics rest in the crypt of the cathedral in Freising, in a golden casket standing on the original sarcophagus of the saintly bishop and herald of the faith. Corbinian was probably born in the last third of the seventh century near Melun on the Seine River in France, the son of an Irish mother and a Frankish father. At first he lived as a hermit near the church of his native place, while his reputation for holiness spread throughout the land. Around the year 710, he undertook a pilgrimage to Rome, where Pope Constantine I consecrated him a bishop and gave him permission to preach. Around 714, he came on his pilgrimage to the city of the popes through Bavaria, where Duke Grimoald would gladly have kept him on as bishop. In fact, Corbinian settled in Freising on his return and began successful mission work among the people, who for the most part were still pagans. Among other things, he dedicated one church in honor of Saint Stephen, alongside of which the famous monastery, Abtei Weihenstephan, was founded. The herald of the faith was highly esteemed, and the duke, too, was well disposed toward him, until Corbinian rebuked him for his illicit marriage with a blood relative. For fear of his revenge, the Bishop had to flee and lived

at first in the monastery of Kains near Meran, until Grimoald died and
his successor, Hugibert, brought him back to Freising. The saint was
welcomed enthusiastically by the people but died shortly afterward, prob-
ably around 728. At his request, his remains were laid to rest first in
Kains but then were translated to Freising by one of his successors,
Bishop Arbeo, on November 20, 765.

That autumn the *gymnasium* had opened again, and by December the seminary, too, was sufficiently restored to continue its
work and house students. So the rector invited us to come back.
Although both of us had already completed school, we gladly
helped and assisted and used the time to prepare ourselves for
our approaching theology studies. At that time, the pastor of the
parish in Haslach—Stefan Blum was his name—loaned my brother,
who was starving for reading material, a whole series of books
about theology and philosophy, so that he could get something
of a head start in those subjects. Indeed, before the war he had
also urged my brother to transfer to the minor seminary because
he recognized his talent and his vocation.

At Christmas 1945, a class reunion took place in the house of
one of the nonseminarian classmates. Many of our former fellow students who had come through the war unscathed attended.
A number of them told that their parents were now saying they
too had seen that everything would end this way; that it had
been completely clear the war could not be won, but they had
never expressed this openly, so that none of their children would
let it slip out. From a certain point in time on, it was unmis-
takable that Hitler would lose the war. Yet at that time, many
simply did not have the courage to speak openly about it in
their family circle at least. Since there was no public transportation at the time, we remained together the whole night "chatting", until we went home again the next morning.

In December, also, a letter arrived in the mail from Freising
informing us that the major seminary there was going to reopen.

The *Alumnatskurs*, that is, the degree course—today it is called
the pastoral course—had already begun in November. So on January 3, 1946, we were able to familiarize ourselves with our
new seminary and four days later to begin our studies at the
college. Because of the war, my brother and I were now in the
same situation. Neither of us had an *Abitur* [the examination
qualifying a student for university]; we had only a diploma—
today one would say we had finished eleventh grade with a certificate of matriculation. With that, one was allowed to study at
a college or a university; however, we had to make up several
courses, as determined by the competent dean of studies. This
was handled in a very humane way. Naturally we had to enroll
in a Latin course, in which we translated hymns from the Breviary, and take some remedial Greek—in that class we read the
New Testament in the original—and also complete courses in
secular history—the name of the subject in the curriculum in
those days time was "profane history"—and biology. At that time,
much more attention was given to these secular subjects at a
theological college than today. And then it started!

*The Archdiocesan Major Seminary in Freising had also served during
World War II as a military hospital for wounded prisoners of war from
many countries and likewise had to be put back in order before it could
open its doors to the newly enrolled candidates for the priesthood. Only
after the discharge of some of the wounded did rooms become available
again; at the start of the new year 1946, then, there was finally space
for all the candidates.*

*While large sectors of Munich had been destroyed by the hail of
Allied bombs, the "cathedral hill" (Domberg) of Freising and its famous
Marian church had been spared. Nevertheless, conditions were Spartan
by today's standards, and the seminarians were housed in an extremely
restricted space. Most of them had to spend the night in dormitories and
stayed in the study halls during the day; there was no opportunity to
withdraw into a private place, and the strict house rules allowed only a*

little freedom. But that did not bother the young men. After years of war and Nazi terror, they were grateful to be able finally to pursue their vocation.

As we entered the seminary building, a young man wearing a white "Roman collar" (a characteristic sign of a cleric) crossed our path; he was carrying a whole stack of books, which he held down with his chin so they did not fall to the floor. Immediately we knew we were in the right place. We mistook him at first for a priest, but later we learned he had not yet been ordained a priest but was a seminarian in his final year of coursework. At any rate, we walked into a large room that had originally served as a banquet hall (and today once again has this function), the so-called "Red Hall", which is famous for its valuable paintings from Tyrol. At that time, however, it had been converted into a large study hall. It was filled with several dozen beginning students who, like us, had come there to study theology. They were to become the "legendary" first postwar generation of priests in Freising.

Gathered together in that place were about 120 men who could not have been more different—and yet all of them were inspired by the desire to become a priest. The ages ranged from not-yet-nineteen-year-olds, like Joseph Ratzinger, to almost-forty-year-olds. Many of the more mature men had been through the whole war, had fought at the front and experienced its horrors firsthand. They had gone through trials and endured dark nights of suffering that had marked them deeply. To them, the younger seminarians seemed like immature children who lacked any depth of experience—in their opinion, the soil in which an authentic response to a priestly vocation had to develop. Nevertheless, they were all united in their gratitude for having survived those difficult years and in their enormous resolve to make up finally for what they had missed. They had become witnesses to the truth of Christ's prophecy to Peter that not even the gates of hell could prevail against his Church. The

Brownshirt regime had tried in vain to destroy them. Even in the days of darkest gloom, the Church had proved to be the place of their hopes. Despite all her human weaknesses, she had become the counterbalance to the demonic ideology of National Socialism. The task that now lay ahead was to make the faith a basis for a better Germany and ultimately for a better world.

An advanced seminarian who had already completed most of his studies became our "prefect", as we used to say then, in other words, our tutor. His name was Alfred Läpple, and he was later professor of catechetics and religious education and also dean of the Theology Faculty at the University of Salzburg.

In 1939, Alfred Läpple (b. 1915) needed only a few more months to complete his studies at the University of Munich. Läpple was already working on his dissertation when the Nazis closed the Theology Faculty in retaliation against the Archbishop of Munich, Michael Cardinal von Faulhaber. He was then drafted into the military, served in the air force, and was present at the occupation of the Baltic states and also on the Russian front. Finally, he ended up in Westphalia as an American prisoner of war and was sent to a gigantic POW camp near Le Havre in France. His language skills were helpful to him there: he made himself useful as a translator for the camp administration and convinced them to accommodate the three hundred or so Catholic priests from among the almost 500,000 prisoners in a separate block and to offer theological lectures for them. Not until November 1945 did he return to bombed-out Munich, where he learned that the seminary program had just been reinstated in Freising.

In an interview with the magazine 30 Days *(1/2006) Professor Läpple reminisced about that time. "I called the Freising seminary to learn what to do. I had spoken with the new rector, Michael Höck. . . . He had been my prefect of studies at the junior seminary. . . . He said: Dear Alfred, I was expecting you, I have a fine job for you. You're to be prefect of studies for the new men, those who have never been in seminary. I went, and he led me into the largest room (roter Saal) in the seminary, which was usually opened only for solemn celebrations. They had arranged desks and chairs, and there were sixty beginners. Rector Höck told them: Dear boys, here's the best man I've found for you, you'll be well off with him. Among those sixty boys there were also the two Ratzinger brothers. A few days later, during a break, this young man approached me, whom I still didn't know. He said: I am Joseph Ratzinger, and I have some questions for you. From those questions our first work together arose. And it was the beginning of many conversations, of many walks, of many impassioned discussions and of many works done together."* In the same interview, Professor Läpple also recalled the first question the young Joseph Ratzinger asked him: *"How did you manage to keep the faith during all the time of the war?"* His answer must have impressed the young seminarian: *"I told him that it had been my mother's prayers. . . . And that I knew that Christ loved me, and if I was spared, then it would be Christ who would consume my life."*

"He was like a dry [sponge] soaking up water almost greedily", Läpple described his first impression of the young candidate for the priesthood, who was to become pope someday. *"When in his studies he came across something new, that could correct or open new paths in terms of what he already knew, he was full of enthusiasm."*

We took a liking to Läpple from the start. He was self-assured and sociable and always spoke what was in his heart. He always gave us a whole series of lessons, at least one per day, usually in the early morning, even before breakfast or else right afterward. We liked him very much and appreciated him academically, too. We knew he would earn a doctorate. At first he had been a student of Professor Theodor Steinbüchel (*1888–1949*), who taught in Munich before the war and then went to Tübingen in 1941. His former teacher had also suggested the topic of his dissertation, *The Individual in the Church: Characteristics of a Theology of the Individual according to John Henry Cardinal Newman,* which he submitted in 1952. Since then he has written a great deal, more than 150 publications, which have been translated into many languages. In this he was helped by the fact that he had a great gift for languages; simply put, he was a very special man.

Yet the rector of the major seminary, who addressed the introductory remarks to us, impressed us also. Doctor Michael Höck had spent many years in the Dachau concentration camp. As editor-in-chief of the church newspaper, he had had a public profile as an enlightened opponent of the Nazis and had written things that did not sit well with the regime. He was a very kindly man who was always concerned about us, and we all held him in high esteem. Therefore at the seminar everybody called him "Vater Höck".

Doctor Michael Höck (1903–1996) had studied at the Germanicum in Rome by the good offices of the Archbishop of Munich, Michael Cardinal von Faulhaber, and was ordained a priest there in 1930. When he returned to Germany the following year, the Cardinal appointed him prefect of the Archdiocesan Minor Seminary in Freising. In addition, Höck was appointed editor-in-chief of the Münchener Katholische Kirchenzeitung *in 1934. Again and again he expressed "between the lines" his objections to the Nazi regime, which led to various clashes with the Gestapo and repeated confiscations of the church newspaper. In April 1940, the paper was finally forbidden, and Höck was put on trial. Although the court exonerated him, the Gestapo arrested him shortly thereafter and whisked him away, first to a prison in Berlin for interrogation, then to the Oranienburg concentration camp, and finally, together with the future Auxiliary Bishop Johannes Neuhäusler and the Evangelical Lutheran theologian Martin Niemöller, to the dreaded Dachau concentration camp. There he stayed and suffered until the liberation of the camp by the Americans in April 1945.*

The vice-rector was our former chaplain in Traunstein, a late-vocation priest by the name of Baumgartner; our instructor for the history of philosophy was a Professor Fellermeier; and the cathedral choirmaster's name was Franz Xaver Geisenhofer. Also in our seminary was the future Cardinal Leo Scheffczyk (*1920–2005*). He was from Upper Silesia and had already studied Catholic theology at the University of Breslau before the war; he then completed his studies with us in Freising. He was together with Läpple in the *Alumnatskurs* that the advanced students attended. Besides that, there were three other theological and two philosophical courses of studies, the latter for us beginners. Scheffczyk seemed to us at first a bit conceited, but as we got to know him better, we noticed that he was not vain at all; he was just shy and somewhat lacking in self-confidence. It happens rather often in life that timidity is mistaken for conceitedness. At any rate, he preached interesting sermons that fascinated us, and he could sing very well—he had a wonderful high tenor voice. Later he became a great theologian and a world-renowned Mariologist, whom Pope John Paul II raised to the rank of cardinal in his last consistory in appreciation of his services.

Another unusual fellow student was Matthias Defregger (*1915–1995*), a grandson of the famous painter Franz von Defregger, who later became Vicar General of the Archdiocese of Munich and then Auxiliary Bishop. Apparently he had lost his parents at an early age and liked to tell stories about his mother, a fashion designer from France, who must have been a very interesting woman. In the military, he had been promoted to the rank of Major and was therefore a high-ranking officer, which is why there were rumors about him after the war. And so I could name them one after the other and tell how they all later found their place in life in one way or another.

We immediately felt comfortable in this circle. Yes, and then the coursework really got started! Early in the morning, Mass and meditation in the seminary chapel led off the daily routine. Breakfast followed, and then classes began. In the afternoon, after

Joseph Ratzinger (to the far right of the altar) serving Mass

the midday meal, further lectures and seminars were held. Sunday Mass was not celebrated in the seminary chapel but, rather, in the Freising cathedral, which for us was always an especially valuable opportunity and a wonderful spiritual experience.

At other times, some of us were accommodated in rooms with ten to fifteen beds, while others had smaller rooms with fewer beds; my brother and I usually slept in different rooms. The rooms were unheated, and in winter it was bitter cold. The wash water that had already been set out in the evening was then covered in the morning with a thin crust of ice that we first had to break.

One roommate of the future pope in Freising was Pavlo Kohut (1926–2006), a Ukrainian Greek Catholic who had fled to Germany from the Russians and now wanted to become a priest. When I interviewed Father Kohut in the summer of 2005, he no longer recalled where he had met Joseph Ratzinger for the first time, in the study hall or at a meal. Yet he still remembered vividly the impression he had of him: "I knew right away: this is a man who is not your peer, he is something quite special. He immediately took an interest in me and listened to me attentively. That meant a great deal to me in my situation at the time. As time went on, we became better acquainted and often went on walks together. I told him about my youth, my uncle, my parents, and about the fact that it was not possible for me to learn anything about them because of the political situation. The Iron Curtain had closed; it was impossible to send letters or receive news reports. He immediately offered to help me in my difficult situation, for which I am still grateful to him today. At that time I had some problems with the German language. He helped me to write letters, complete assignments, and corrected the results. He always looked after me, and you could tell that he did it gladly. He was never imposing, he was always very restrained. He was never full of self-importance, as is sometimes the case with young people, and he did not make himself the center of attention. . . . In everything he did, he showed the utmost concentration—whether he was studying, working, or talking with me, he never let himself be distracted by something else. He learned constantly; he was constantly hungry for new knowledge. Whenever I saw him, he was reading; he used every minute to learn. And he was always very orderly, very well organized. As you see, his diligence paid off."

I myself did not have much contact with Pavlo Kohut, but my brother was very good friends with him. He was a very sociable, nice man, and everyone knew that he came from the Eastern Church, about which he could tell us a lot. So he was generally well liked, and all of us had good memories of him.

Above all, the candidates for the priesthood who had now returned home were hungry for learning and knowledge. After the dullness of the war years and the monotonous subjection to Brownshirt propaganda, they hungered and thirsted for literature, which helped them cope with what they had experienced and find answers to the questions that occupied their inmost thoughts.

First and foremost was the question of guilt. What sins of omission had led to a situation in which the brown pied pipers were able to come into power? What share did they themselves have in the responsibility for the atrocities of the regime? How could men be capable of such things at all? Where was God; why had he remained silent? Had he long since forgotten men, or were they the ones who had turned their back on him? How could one show remorse and do penance for what had happened? And, above all, how could citizens make sure that the horrors of National Socialism could never be repeated? The seminarians read Gertrud von le Fort, Ernst Wiechert, and Dostoyevsky, whose novel Crime and Punishment *went to the heart of the central question of those days; they flocked to the lectures of the moral theologian Steinbüchel, who introduced them to the philosophers Heidegger and Jaspers. Steinbüchel's book* Der Umbruch des Denkens *(The revolution of thought) became key reading for Joseph Ratzinger, who made the title his motto. That was just what Germany, what the world needed now—a 180-degree turn back to God! Everyone had had an all-too-drastic experience of what happens when a society separates itself from God and declares man the measure of all things and master of life and death.*

In order to distinguish between us, our fellow students called us "Bücher-Ratz" (Bookish-Ratz), which of course was my brother, and "Orgel-Ratz" (Organ-Ratz), since I was more interested in music. In Freising we had the seminary library, a reference library, and finally the cathedral library, so really there was no shortage of books for him. He always read everything he considered worth reading. At that time, the custom was that when a priest had died, his library would be brought to the seminary. There the students who staffed the library culled anything that was still missing in the collection or might be valuable, and the rest was auctioned off among us seminarians. So we bought all sorts of valuable things at auction. For there were scarcely any books on sale at that time, and then they were printed on very cheap paper and were rather expensive.

I cannot remember all the things we used to read in those days. The works by Alois Dempf about the philosophy of history were of course in use. Then the books by Romano Guardini, for instance, *Sacred Signs* and, naturally, his important book on Christ, *The Lord*. Many enjoyed reading Michael Schmaus' *Christus das Urbild des Menschen* (Christ, the archetype of man), but also Joseph Bernhart's *Der Kaplan* (The parish priest)—unfamiliarity with that work was considered to be almost a gap in one's education. Bernhart (*1881–1969*) was a Swabian from Bavaria who had studied theology and taken an advanced degree before he was assigned to be an assistant pastor in a little village. He was bored there and became acquainted with a woman, fell in love with her, and even married her, which of course meant that he left the priesthood. For a time he was even excommunicated. During that critical time in his life, he wrote the aforementioned book. He later became a philosopher of religion and an author and published something about the *Summa theologica* by Thomas Aquinas—not an academic book, but a popularization for a wider public, written in a wonderful, very polished style and on a high level theologically, which we appreciated very much.

In the library there were also books listed on the "Index of Forbidden Books". They had been collected in a special bookcase that was usually locked, which we called "the poison cabinet". *Der Kaplan*, which of course I read, too, was in it; other than that, not too much from that collection, because after all I spent a great deal of time practicing at the piano and the organ. My brother was different that way; he could never read enough.

Yet while he was scaling the loftiest heights of philosophy and theology, Joseph Ratzinger always remained connected with the faith of his childhood. That, too, was a result of the experience with National Socialism. "In the faith of my parents I found the confirmation that Catholicism had been a bulwark of truth and justice against that regime of atheism and falsehood" (ST 56), he later wrote. It was a faith that had stood the test in the darkest hour of history. So, on the one hand, he discussed with his fellow seminarians the great Doctors of the Church, but he nevertheless remained a man of simple, downright rural piety. He highly esteemed Bishop Augustine of Hippo (354–430), a man of artistic sensibility and ardent passion, who also lived in a time of radical change, namely, the era of mass migration; he discovered that contemporary man can also identify with this "suffering, questioning man" (SE 61). He preferred "flesh and blood" theologians to lofty theoreticians. And he wholeheartedly agreed with Augustine that one cannot become a Christian by birth but only through inner conversion.

My brother was enthusiastic about Saint Augustine from the start, even though we never spoke directly about it. No doubt this great Doctor of the Church is a fascinating phenomenon simply because of the depth of his ideas, but also because of his voluminous works. One key work, his autobiography, as it were, is of course *The Confessions*, in which he gives evidence about his life, which was by no means honorable in every respect and yet led him through many detours to Christ and his Church. Indeed, he initially led a rather materialistic life and then joined an elite sect. Only later, after countless prayers of his mother, Monica, did he meet Saint Ambrose of Milan and accept the Catholic faith. Then, of course, we should mention *De civitate Dei, The City of God*, his outline of an ideal society; his study of the Blessed Trinity, *De Trinitate*, which is considered his theological masterpiece, and also *De doctrina christiana* (which we also read), which contains a sort of theory of teaching Church doctrine.

Naturally we were all interested in that, but only Joseph really took the time to deal with special topics above and beyond the assigned reading. In contrast, I used to read whatever was directly connected with the lectures and what was required for the examinations.

Especially the first exams after the war were rather suspenseful, since for some seminarians, after all those years at the front, the academic routine was an entirely new situation that seemed quite unfamiliar.

I can still remember very well one of them who came from Engelsberg (near Garching) and so was a real warhorse, who in the military nonetheless had made first lieutenant. Beforehand, he used to say, "Gentlemen, we have been through a lot already, and no one thought anything of it, and now at exam time you are trembling!" He thought it rather undignified to be afraid of tests. And so for his first exam he went quite cheerfully into the examination room, having previously taken a shot of the liquor his parents had distilled. Therefore he already had some blood alcohol content. He went through the door and left it open, so we too could hear what happened there in the professor's room. He related things we had never heard before! Finally our philosophy professor, Jakob Fellermeier, who always spoke somewhat stiltedly, although he came from a very simple Bavarian farming family, declared to him: "Well, that was nothing special, I do have to tell you, and strictly speaking I could not let you pass at all, but since you were a combatant for so many years during the war, I will let that suffice for now. . . ." Then we noticed that the two men were afraid of each other: the professor, that this old warrior would become violent and do him harm, and the other, that the professor would flunk him.

It was like that with another ex-soldier from the vicinity of Waging, also a thickheaded farm boy, who was not very interested in philosophy and studied only what was absolutely necessary in theology. Then in his exam with our philosophy professor Johann Nepomuk Espenberger, he knew so little that the latter was beside himself and could only stammer in his best Bavarian dialect: "*Ja, Herr Kandidat,* Mr. Candidate, what am I going to do? That really wasn't very bright, it wasn't bright at all. What

am I going to do? I'll give you a two; are you happy with that?"
Of course he was happy.

Our first examination, therefore, was for all concerned a big
adventure; those stalwart, brawny guys had already gone through
all sorts of things in military operations when they were soldiers, and they were most certainly not squeamish. But since
they now had to cram and reproduce so much knowledge as
answers to rather difficult questions, many of them were simply
overwhelmed. Thank God everything went well, both for them
and for our professors!

It was something quite special when Cardinal Faulhaber visited
the major seminary in Freising. You could tell it from the meal alone;
we would stand there in the refectory, facing the cross, and behind
us was the "head table", at which the Cardinal, too, was supposed
to sit. Attentive silence prevailed in the hall when we suddenly heard
his footsteps approaching. Then the Cardinal, his secretary, the
rector, and the other dignitaries came in, and of course we turned
around to see him. He always impressed us enormously; he was a
phenomenon that automatically instilled respect. That was already
the case in Tittmoning, when we were only little and saw him for
the first time; but now, as grown men, we still felt the same reverence for that man. Meanwhile, we had both been confirmed by
him also, I in 1935 at the age of eleven, and my brother three years
later. But only now did we sense also the burden of sufferings that
weighed upon him, for he had gone through a difficult time during National Socialism.

*Michael Cardinal von Faulhaber (1869–1952) came from Lower Fran-
conia and was the son of a baker and farmer. After his studies and a
professorship at the University of Strasbourg, he was consecrated Bishop
of Speyer in 1911. In 1913, Prince-Regent Ludwig III of Bavaria
raised him to the rank of nobility. This was followed in 1917 by his
appointment as Archbishop of Munich and Freising, and four years
later Pope Benedict XV summoned him to the College of Cardinals.*

As a Bavarian loyal to the king, he took a critical stance vis-à-vis the Weimar Republic, but he wholeheartedly rejected National Socialism. In 1930, he described it as a "heresy" that could "not be reconciled with Christian doctrine". He reacted to the Nazis' anti-Semitic agitation as early as 1923,[1] but also in 1933 with sermons in the cathedral in Munich, in which he emphasized that the Christian faith is rooted in Judaism. In 1926, he joined the "Amici Israel", a group of high-ranking Catholic clerics and theologians who were striving for a Christian-Jewish reconciliation, and ordered his priests in their sermons to avoid anything "that sounded anti-Semitic". Even his episcopal coat of arms expressed this message. It showed the dove, the Holy Spirit, lighting the menorah, the seven-branched candlestick of the Jews—symbolizing the presence of the Holy Spirit even in the Old Testament, in Judaism. He explicitly supported the Catholic journalist Fritz Michael Gerlich, publisher of Der Gerade Weg *and the strongest voice warning against the Nazis. As a close confidant of the apostolic nuncio in Bavaria at the time, the Cardinal Secretary of State, Eugenio Pacelli (later Pope Pius XII), in 1937, he composed the original text of the encyclical* Mit brennender Sorge, *in which Pope Pius XI would condemn National Socialism with a severity that is unique in papal documents of the modern era. In 1934, the Nazis made an attempt on Faulhaber's life, followed in 1938 by an attack on the Archbishop's palace, after it became known that he had offered shelter to the chief rabbi of Munich during the Kristallnacht and had allowed him to hide the precious Torah scrolls from the synagogue in his residence. Even though from time to time he also had strived for mediation and moderation and was even willing to have a dialogue with Adolf Hitler, he never allowed himself to be exploited*

---

[1] On November 14, 1923, Archbishop Eugenio Pacelli, the future Pope Pius XII, who was at that time apostolic nuncio in Munich, reported to the Vatican Secretariat of State about "the anti-Catholic character of the Nazi uprising in Munich". Singling out for mention "Hitler and Ludendorff, the stars among the street orators", Pacelli noted that "the particular target of the attacks was the learned and conscientious Cardinal Archbishop, who in a sermon in the cathedral on the fourth of this month had denounced the persecution of the Jews.... So it happened that during the riots last Saturday afternoon [the armed uprising by Hitler on November 11, 1923—Ed.] a large group of demonstrators marched up in front of the Archiepiscopal palace and shouted, 'Down with the Cardinal!'"

by the Brownshirt dictators. In 1940, in a public letter to the Minister of Justice of the Reich, he condemned the mass killing of the handicapped; in 1941, he publicly spoke out against the removal of crucifixes from the schools; in 1943, together with the other German bishops, he protested against the murder of people of other races and ancestry. This man of God, one of the last great princes of the Church in Germany, remained an imposing figure for his entire life; after the war, he led efforts to alleviate the sufferings of the populace and to distribute the humanitarian aid that Pope Pius XII generously placed at his disposal. "What moved me deeply about him was the awe-inspiring grandeur of his mission, with which he had become fully identified" (M 45), Joseph Ratzinger wrote about him in his memoirs.

In the seminary many stories were told about him. One time the janitor, who also served at meals, inadvertently spilled gravy on his cassock. Then the Cardinal looked at him reproachfully, while the janitor, Herr Bartl, just stammered, "It doesn't matter, Your Eminence, we still have enough gravy out in the kitchen."

One day we met him in the corridor of the seminary, and the rector was there too, who introduced us to him. He then spoke just a few words to us, very slowly and with an emphatic intonation. For us, though, it was as if we had met the dear Lord in person, his appearance was so dignified. At that time he still wore on liturgical occasions a large train about 23 feet long, the so-called *cappa magna*, and during his visits one of us was designated to carry that train, to which we replied, "ad caudam", in other words, "at the train". It was a great honor to be assigned to this duty "ad caudam" by our prefect for liturgy, and a few times my brother was chosen for it. We all admired him, and some also envied him, that he was allowed to carry the Cardinal's train. But for me there was never any question of that; I had no time at all for it; after all, I had to sing in the men's choir whenever the Lord Cardinal came to visit.

*With the summer semester in 1947, the two-year program of philos-
ophy studies in Freising ended for the brothers. For his theology studies, Joseph Ratzinger transferred to the University of Munich, where
the theological faculty had at that time been relocated in the former
royal hunting lodge at Fürstenried. There the seminarians and staff
lived, taught, and studied in extremely confined quarters, and occasionally he felt as though he had returned to the Flak battery. One
and the same building housed the living quarters for two professors,
the administrative office and the meeting room of the faculty, three
seminary libraries, and the study halls and dormitories of the students,
who slept in bunk beds. The food, too, was meager, because they
could not rely on a farm belonging to the seminary as in Freising.
The lectures took place in the greenhouse, which in the winter was
ice-cold and in the summer scorching hot. A large, beautiful park on
the castle grounds, however, which was laid out partly in the English
style and partly in the French manner, compensated for the inconve-
niences. There Ratzinger could walk for hours, immerse himself in his
thoughts, and arrive at important decisions.*

In 1947, we both took the examination in philosophy and received
the *admissio*, which made us candidates for the priesthood. My
brother then went to Munich together with two other seminarians, our "compatriot" from Traunstein, Rupert Berger, and Hans
Finkenzeller. All the others, myself included, remained in Freising.

*The reason for the change was obvious: despite the wretched conditions,
renowned professors who had come from all parts of the country taught
in Fürstenried: Professors Stummer, Maier, and Seppelt from Breslau,
Egenter from Braunsberg, Söhngen from Cologne, Schmaus, Pascher,
and Mörsdorf from Münster. They were the best theologians of their
time, and Joseph Ratzinger listened to them with enthusiasm. "I found
it wonderful", he recalled. "Broad horizons of thought and faith opened
up before me, and I was learning to ponder the primordial questions of
human existence, the questions of my own life" (SE 55).*

Here the foundation for his own theology developed, the basic ele-
ments of which are Sacred Scripture and the Fathers of the Church. Yet
he never wanted to "stop short in the ancient Church". Rather, his
constant concern was to "get below the encrustations, to expose the real
kernel of the faith, and thus give it fresh power and dynamism" (ST 58).
In 1950 he took part in a competition that was sponsored each year by
the faculty. The theme was: "The People and the House of God in
Augustine's Doctrine of the Church".

That happened in his last year of studies, at the end of his
third year of theology. The professors took turns, and each
year one of them held the competition and challenged the students to submit anonymously a major study on one theme or
another. The one who produced the best work not only received
a modest sum of money, but more importantly his written work
was accepted as a dissertation. As luck would have it, that year
it was the turn of a professor whom my brother esteemed very
highly and with whom he would gladly have worked on his
dissertation anyway, namely, Doctor Gottlieb Söhngen (*1892–*
1971). The professor himself encouraged him to take the opportunity that was presenting itself, and I too urged him. Therefore,
during his *alumnat*, his last year of studies, he worked very
hard and diligently on it, using every free minute to study
Augustine's works and to read the works of other theologians
who dealt with the writings of that great Doctor of the Church.
So he was able to complete that study in only nine months. It
proved to be a real challenge, incidentally, since, in addition,
we were supposed to be ordained to the subdiaconate and the
diaconate at the end of October, which began our preparation
for the priesthood. That, too, was connected with intensive
preparations and spiritual exercises that required a lot of time.
My sister and I, therefore, made an effort to spare Joseph as
much work as possible. I took care of all the practical necessi-
ties, while Maria, who was employed as a secretary in a law

office, typed a clean copy of his manuscript. In that way it was possible to submit it right before the deadline.

Of course, Joseph Ratzinger's study won the competition. He thereby had not only handed in his dissertation but also convinced his doctoral advisor of his mettle. His former prefect Alfred Läpple, who had long since become one of his best friends, remembers that, after Ratzinger wrote the work about Augustine, "[Söhngen] said: 'Now my student knows more than [I] who am teacher!' . . . He once said he felt like Albertus Magnus, when in the Middle Ages he declared that his student would make more noise than [he]. And the student was Thomas [Aquinas]!" (30 D).

Yet in spite of all his enthusiasm, there were doubts, also. Joseph Ratzinger was fascinated by academic theology, of that he was certain. But would he also be of any use as a priest? "Since I was rather diffident and downright unpractical, since I had no talent for sports or administration or organization, I had to ask myself whether I would be able to relate to people", he admitted to the journalist Peter Seewald (SE 55). Would he be able as a chaplain to lead and inspire Catholic youth? Would he be capable of giving religious instruction to children? Would he be able to get along with the elderly and the sick? "I had to ask myself whether I would be ready to do that my whole life long and whether it was really my vocation" (SE 56). Celibacy, too, caused him some concern. In Fürstenried, not only did the students and the professors live in very close quarters, but also male and female students. The female sex had its attraction, even though Joseph would never have dared to begin a relationship. Yet at some time or other came the moment when the doubts abruptly fled. The future Pope Benedict XVI said: "I was convinced, I myself don't know how, that God wanted something from me that could be attained only by my becoming a priest" (SE 53–54). With his diaconal ordination in the autumn of 1950, he then definitively said his Yes with conviction to God's plan for him. In order to be introduced to the practical aspects of the priestly vocation as well, he went back to his brother at the major seminary in Freising. In their final year, the two candidates for the priesthood listened to lectures on pastoral theology given by the rector, Father Höck, on liturgical praxis by the vice-rector, Father Braun, on the administration of the sacraments by Alfred Läpple, and on homiletics by the Augustinian priest Father Gabriel Schlachter. Furthermore, the cathedral choirmaster, Max Eham, instructed them in Gregorian chant. That academic class produced three bishops: besides Joseph Ratzinger, also Franz Xaver Schwarzenböck (1923–2010) and Heinrich Graf Soden-Fraunhofen (1920–2000), both of whom were consecrated bishops in 1972 (five years before Ratzinger).

Of course, all of us had our doubts here and there, whether we would be up to the demands of a priestly vocation, whether we could really tackle the job. It is easier today, because now there is a pastoral year in which a candidate for the priesthood can already acquire some initial experience in a parish. That was not yet the case with us; we still had no practical experience whatsoever in pastoral care.

As far as celibacy is concerned, that was part of our life decision from the beginning. In the minor seminary, it was already clear to us that we wanted to become priests, and they are unmarried. Of course we were aware of that from the start; we had maintained this point of view throughout our adult life, and so the obligation we assumed when we were ordained deacons was not especially difficult for us.

What *was* new, actually, was our obligation to pray the Breviary, which is very extensive and was even more extensive then than today. That meant a time-consuming prayer obligation that considerably transformed our life and our daily routine.

Then the great day drew near, the most important one in the lives of the Ratzinger brothers: on Friday, June 29, 1951, Joseph and Georg Ratzinger were ordained priests by Michael Cardinal von Faulhaber in the cathedral in Freising. It was a brilliant summer day when the forty-four candidates were to pronounce their "Adsum"—"Here I am!" Then

The priests ordained in 1951 in the Archdiocese of Munich and Freising.
Fourth row from the top, fourth from the left: Joseph Ratzinger. First row, far
right: Georg Ratzinger.

when the aged Archbishop, who was already at the twilight of his life, imposed his hands on Joseph Ratzinger, a twittering lark flew from the high altar up into the cathedral cupola. For the young priest, it was a sign, an encouragement from on high, that he was on the right path. On one of the two prayer cards commemorating his First Mass, however, was printed the appropriate quotation from Saint Paul: "Not that we are sufficient of ourselves to claim anything as coming from us; our sufficiency is from God" [2 Cor 3:5].

Naturally we were rather excited. We did not want to leave anything to chance. So already on the evening before, we shined our shoes and prepared our clothes. I do not recall how we spent the morning hours, but I still remember well how we vested and walked in solemn procession from the seminary to the cathedral. Of course, this took place in a very special emotional state, for it was a solemn feast day for us, actually the high point of our lives. The streets were decorated with banners, and the whole city seemed to be on foot, the event was so solemn.

As we entered the cathedral, the organ thundered and the men's choir sang. Our liturgy provides us with such wonderful experiences! There was standing room only in the cathedral; the people literally thronged to participate in this special event, our ordination to the priesthood. Of course, our parents and our sister, Maria, had come to Freising for this important occasion, and many of our friends as well. The sound of the organ and the splendid colors of the flowers decorating the church did their part to intensify the already festive mood and to lend an additional, sensory dimension to it. Then the ordination rite was celebrated, in a form that was very moving to us at the time. The high point of it was the Litany of the Saints, during which we lay on the floor before the altar and in that posture prayed and sang along in complete abandonment to God. Everyone present, even our teachers and the assembled laity, joined in, so

The brothers Joseph (left) and Georg (middle) Ratzinger with their friend Rupert Berger at the welcome ceremony in their home parish in Traunstein after their priestly ordination

as to implore for us the help of all the saints in heaven in preparation for our ordination. Thus we became more profoundly certain that with the imposition of hands by the Archbishop, a new chapter of our life was beginning that would be pleasing to God and rich in blessings.

My brother recounted later that at the imposition of hands, that is, at the actual moment of ordination, he saw a little bird that soared from the high altar into the cupola and warbled a song. I must admit I did not notice that, but I know he is more sensitive to such occurrences in creation. Perhaps it really was a sign that God's blessing was upon him.

At the end of the ordination rite, each of us carried forward a lighted candle that he gave to the Archbishop, while a special hymn was intoned by the choir. This ritual, which no longer exists today, moved us deeply at the time. The offering of the candle symbolized once again our own life, which we were giving away so that the light of the Gospel might burn and illuminate the world. It was the moving conclusion of a ceremony through which our whole life was renewed. For what can be more beautiful than to come before the living God and to serve him—and thereby to serve mankind as well? At that time, on the evening of ordination day, a solemn farewell reception was also held for the newly ordained priests in the minor

The most important moment in the life of the future pope: Cardinal Faulhaber imposes hands on him.

seminary beside the cathedral, which today is the diocesan museum. But unfortunately we could not attend it. We had to travel home on the same day as our ordination, because two days later one of our closest friends (*the future liturgist and pastoral theologian*) Rupert Berger (*b. 1926*), the son of the mayor of Traunstein, was celebrating his First Mass, and we had promised him that we would serve as deacon and subdeacon at it.

Our own First Mass took place one week later, on July 8, likewise in the parish church of Saint Oswald in Traunstein. Since there was no concelebration in those days, each of us had to celebrate his own First Mass, my brother in the early morning at 7:00, and I two hours later at 9:00. The early Mass was a Mass with congregational singing; the 9:00 Mass was a Solemn High Mass. My brother said that I should take that one, since I was well acquainted with the church choir, whereas he was willing to celebrate even the somewhat less solemn liturgy.

The evening before, the youth choir of the parish in Traunstein performed in Hufschlag especially for us; a friend of ours directed the group, which sang several songs. When they had finished, our pastor, Father Els, climbed up on a table and gave a fiery speech. His first name was Georg, and we always used to call him "Rocket-George", and before that "Express-George" also, because he was incredibly fast in everything that he did, even in celebrating Mass: no sooner had he closed the tabernacle door than he was already giving the final blessing, often while still on the steps to the altar. "Out of hard stone," he began, meaning Hufschlag, which did not have such a good reputation, "a spark has sprung after all"—for this insignificant suburb had just produced two priests! It was a wonderful evening, not hot, but nice and warm; there were wonderful fragrances in the air, and the June beetles flew around us.

"Rocket-George" preached at my brother's First Mass, too. Actually our friend Alfred Läpple was supposed to have done it, but a few days before he had sent us a telegram saying that he could not speak because he had just had surgery to remove part of his jaw. Then our pastor, who was a magnificent preacher himself, said he would take over. As for the music, my brother asked him to select the simplest songs in the hymnal, for the people would at least know them. But Father Els did not agree with that at all; he wanted something more solemn and decided on the *Mass of Christ the King* by Josef Haas. Haas was president of the music college in Munich, a student of [the composer Max] Reger, and the teacher of my teacher, Höller; therefore I was, so to speak, his "grand-student". He himself had once been a teacher and composed sacred music, including Masses to be sung by the people, such as the aforementioned *Mass of Christ the King*, which is actually a little too difficult for congregational singing. The pastor, however, decided that we would do it, since it is solemn and beautiful. Of course, the people were not able to sing it properly, and even the youth choir failed to learn this composition. Yet before starting his sermon, the pastor interjected an appeal for all the people to be so kind as to sing along: "A couple of sparrows from the church choir are twittering, but that is not singing!" The people did not hold it against him; that was simply his way; he was just a very forthright man, our Rocket-George.

Afterward, we first went back home, where a solemn First Mass procession soon met us and brought us again from our parents' house in Hufschlag down to Traunstein. It was a large procession accompanied by altar servers, a brass band, and a big crowd. This was followed by my First Mass, with the *Lord Nelson Mass* by Haydn—and it was a very splendid ceremony. My former religion teacher, Doctor Hubert Pöhlein, preached. I had asked him ahead of time how long his sermon would last, and he said that, if he did not forget anything, it would be around thirty-five minutes. In fact, it took twenty-five minutes, and so he probably forgot something, without anyone noticing.

The Ratzinger brothers on their First Mass procession through Traunstein in 1951

We were quite amazed at how many people had come. Previously they had explained to us that a bicycle race would take place that same day in Traunstein and that therefore we should not be sad if our First Mass was not that well attended. But later we heard there were scarcely any spectators for the bicycle race because all the people had gone to our First Mass. Back then it was not yet like today.

After the First Mass, we had invited a hundred guests or more to a festive meal at the Sailer-Keller Inn, where they served roast

The brothers Georg and Joseph Ratzinger confer their first blessing

veal. That afternoon, solemn prayers of thanksgiving were on
the agenda. That was when we experienced a nasty surprise.
Whereas in the morning we were blessed with plenty of summer sunshine, the first clouds gathered during the reception, and

it began to thunder; then it rained and, finally, came down in torrents. Of course we were sorry for the guests, although the cooler air after the morning heat was also very pleasant.

In those days, it was the custom with First Masses for people who wanted to receive the new priest's blessing to sign up at the rectory office. Therefore, each of us received a list of all the places we were to visit, and so we spent the next few days calling on all these members of the parish and blessing them.

The blessing of a newly ordained priest is considered something very special. People used to say in Bavaria, "For a blessing after a First Mass, it is worth even wearing out the soles of your shoes."

We were on the move all day, from early morning till late in the evening, and we were cordially welcomed everywhere. In every house, we received a snack and a little money as a gift, but above all it made us happy to see what a grace it was to receive holy orders and to have the privilege of handing this blessing on to the people. Again and again, we experienced how ardently the people waited for the priest, a man who was called by God to serve them.

For the first time, Joseph Ratzinger experienced how fervently people awaited his blessing and what power comes from the sacrament of holy orders. As a young man, what could he have given to those people? Now that he was acting on behalf of Christ, though, it was more than they could comprehend.

It was now evident how true the remark of Saint Paul was, which he wrote on the second prayer card commemorating his First Mass: "Not that we lord it over your faith; [rather] we work with you for your joy" (2 Cor 1:24).

VII
Professor
(1951–1977)

A fter our ordination to the priesthood and the weeks after our First Mass, our ways parted once again, for we had to begin our first assignments as young assistant pastors. At first I went for a month to Grainau (near Garmisch-Partenkirchen), whereas my brother went to Bogenhausen, a district in Munich. Soon after that, I was called to be an instructor for two months at the Archdiocesan Minor Seminary in Freising, where I had the privilege of working closely with cathedral choirmaster Eham, whom I highly respected. But apparently they had greater plans for me. So they made it possible for me to study church music at the Musikhochschule München [Munich Music College], while serving as musician and assistant pastor, at first in Saint Ludwig parish. Naturally, we brothers visited each other often, whenever one of us happened to be free. And even when our meetings became less and less frequent, they were all the more cordial then. Above all, however, we spent our vacations together; no one could take that away from us.

On August 1, 1951, Joseph Ratzinger started his first pastoral ministry as assistant pastor in the Precious Blood parish in Munich. It was located in the district of Bogenhausen, one of the "best neighborhoods" in that city with a million inhabitants, which also included a residential district where intellectuals, artists, and high-ranking officials lived, but also their household help and maids. Other streets lined with apartment houses were home to small businessmen and their employees. The rectory had been built by a famous architect and radiated a certain comfort,

173

even though it was often as busy as a beehive. The heart of the parish, the pastor Max Blumschein, became Ratzinger's model. He taught him that a priest must "glow" interiorly and set an example of what that means. His kindness and inner passion were manifested in a constant willingness to serve. He was always there for the people who needed him, literally until his final breath. He died while bringing the sacraments to a dying person (see M 100).

Joseph Ratzinger needed such an example in order to be able to cope at all with the mountain of new tasks that now presented themselves to him. Since the pastor did not spare himself, the twenty-five-year-old assistant did not want to fall behind him in any way, and so he devoted himself zealously to his duties, which he soon began to enjoy—especially dealing with young people. It did him good, he said, "to step outside the intellectual sphere for a change and to learn to talk with children" (SE 64). The young Ratzinger also had to realize that after the reeducation under Hitler, religion played hardly any role anymore in the lives and thinking of many families. He later wrote up his experiences in an essay entitled "The New Pagans and the Church". Later he recalled, "Soon the work with the children in the school, and the resulting association with their parents, became a great joy to me, and the encounter with different groups of Catholic youth also quickly generated a good feeling of community. To be sure, it also became evident how far removed the world of the life and thinking of many children was from the realities of faith and how little our religious instruction coincided with the actual lives and thinking of our families. Nor could I overlook the fact that the form of youth work, which was simply a continuation of methods developed between the two World Wars, would not be able to deal with the changing circumstances of the world we now lived in: we simply had to look for new forms" (M 101).

In Bogenhausen, Joseph was assistant pastor to Father Blumschein, a very kindly man whom he held in high esteem. He actually felt very much at ease in pastoral work. Above all, religious instruction suited him; he had the gift of presenting even the most difficult subjects so that they could be understood by the simpler children and yet still interested the more demanding students. It gave him great joy. Even though during his first year he already had to take on nineteen sessions a week,[1] he always went gladly into the schools as a religion teacher. Of course he taught different grades, so he could not always present the same material but tried to prepare each session individually. Then he also preached in church, which from the start, however, did not give him much trouble. Every morning he sat for an hour in the confessional, on Saturdays for four hours. Several times a week he rode his bicycle across Munich to funerals, and he celebrated baptisms and weddings. In addition, he was in charge of the youth program in the parish. His good relationship with his pastor, but also the good rectory cook they had there, did their part in making him feel very much at home in Bogenhausen. So eventually it was quite difficult for him to give it all up and to devote himself to scholarly work again when the Archbishop called him a year later to the major seminary in Freising, this time as an instructor and confessor. He would gladly have stayed on in a parish as an assistant pastor.

When he returned to Freising on October 1, 1952, Joseph Ratzinger in fact left his parish community with mixed feelings. The feeling of being needed, the contact with people gave him joy in his priesthood in a more direct way than the rather theoretical job of higher education could. On the other hand, it had always been his desire to investigate the truth further and to continue his theological work. But in Freising, too, he was soon directing a youth group, celebrating liturgies in the cathedral, and sitting in the confessional. He lectured on the role of the sacraments in pastoral work—wherein he could rely entirely on his fresh experiences as an assistant pastor. Furthermore, he was completing his

---

[1] Cardinal Ratzinger's memory of this challenging assignment differs slightly in *Milestones, Memoirs 1927–1977*, trans. Erasmo Leiva-Merikakis (San Francisco: Ignatius Press, 1998), 101, where he specifies that he gave "sixteen hours of religious instruction at five different levels", agreeing that this "obviously required much preparation".—TRANS.

doctoral work. His parents were proud and overjoyed when he came home in July 1953 with a mortarboard and a doctorate in theology.

His academic career did not change him at all as a person. We saw each other then less and less often, and I would have noticed it immediately if he had become different in some way. Our parents thought at first that once he was a professor he would be a bit pompous and talk down to people, but he was never like that; he always remained natural, unlike Professor Fellermeier, for instance, whom we had both experienced and who served as a cautionary example for him. There was not the least bit of that in my brother; even in private conversation, he always spoke his dialect and was quite himself. I can still remember well the ceremony in which he received the doctorate. At that time I was an assistant pastor at Saint Ludwig's in Munich—the church is located right by the university—and of course I was present when the whole process was concluded with a celebration. The university employees, in uniform and each holding a staff, led off, and the rector and the deans were all wearing their robes. The young doctor had to give a lecture and defend his theses, which he had composed in Latin, and all this took place in the auditorium of the university. Our parents and our sister had come, too, and were rather impressed by the festive occasion. Afterward, being a young assistant pastor, I invited them to my lodgings in the rectory, and there was bratwurst and rolls and beer, and it all tasted wonderful to us. The other assistant pastor at my parish, Hans Gradl, a simple, pragmatic man without great theological pretentions, joined us and commented drily with regard to the university initiation of my brother: "And you, Hans, I thought to myself, did you really go to a tree nursery?" [2] This

---

[2] The German *Baumschule* (tree nursery; but literally "tree school") is sometimes used humorously to indicate a less demanding school where backward students might be sent. It is used in this instance in a self-deprecating way by Father Gradl, comparing his own education to the higher level just achieved by Joseph Ratzinger.—TRANS.

midday meal together in my room at the rectory in Saint Ludwig's was a beautiful and happy conclusion to the whole celebration, which somehow put our feet back on the ground after those lofty flights of academic rhetoric.

In 1953, Joseph and I again went on vacation together, this time a journey through Switzerland. As an assistant pastor, I had become acquainted with a young priest who had written his dissertation with Professor Richard Egenter as his advisor. Doctor Franz Böckle (*1921–1991*) was his name. Later, he was called to be professor of moral theology at the University of Bonn and finally became its rector and an advisor to the federal government. This Franz Böckle came from Switzerland, from Glarus; he had gone to school in Chur and had served as an assistant pastor in Zurich, and so he was able to put together for us a wonderful tour of Switzerland. On that trip we went to Zurich, Chur, Fribourg, and many other wonderful places. Once we traveled together with him to Belgium, to Brussels, where he was supposed to give a lecture. Actually, we always spent our vacation in places we wanted to see, where we could become a little better informed and educated.

That same year I traveled with Doctor Böckle and acolytes from our parish to Freising, so as to celebrate with my brother the anniversary of our priestly ordination. While I spent the time with Joseph and our sister, who had also come along, Doctor Böckle looked after the boys.

Then suddenly the telephone rang; my brother answered it, and my sister, who was present, noticed that he became quite pale. Then he offered the telephone to me. I took the receiver and heard the voice of Gradl, the other assistant pastor at my parish, who said, "Listen, I have something unpleasant to tell you. We received a telegram: Your father died." We were all shaken! Evidently the pastor had not dared to make the call himself and instead delegated it to the assistant.

Of course it was clear to us that we had to return home immediately. I asked Böckle, therefore, to look after the acolytes and traveled together with my brother and our sister by train to Traunstein. When we stopped in Bad Endorf, a few stations before Traunstein, our mother suddenly boarded the train. Naturally we went over to her immediately and said, "Mother, we heard that Father died; was he ill?" She was quite exasperated, knew nothing about it, and only reassured us, "No, he was not sick. I left at around noon; he was still well; there was nothing wrong with him at all. We agreed that I would travel to Endorf, and so I did." In Bad Endorf, there is a folk theater that was founded in 1790 and is considered the third oldest theater in Bavaria. There they always performed religious dramas about the lives of the saints, and she had seen one that day.

In Traunstein, we got off the train, quickly took a taxi, and arrived home—and there was Father standing in front of the house, shining his shoes! Good Lord, we certainly were relieved! Then it turned out that his younger brother, Anton, had died, who had once inherited the family farm and had been suffering for a long time from intestinal cancer. His family had informed me by telegram, which simply read: "Our father has died." When the pastor and the assistant opened the telegram in Munich and read it, they no doubt thought that it meant my father, and of course they immediately called my brother's phone number, which I had left with them in case of an emergency. And so we then traveled to Traunstein in a state of great agitation, while our father was at home shining his shoes in peace and quiet!

Naturally he wanted to travel the next day to his brother's funeral. I said to him, "Father, now I am not going to let you go there alone", and I accompanied him on that trip to Rickering, his birthplace. That same day, the clergy of the deanery met at the parish in Schwanenkirchen, and I was also invited to attend. "You sit here", they said, and then a wonderful Bavarian snack was served, which I ate with great relish: smoked meat (bacon), bread and butter, and a beer with it. Things like that leave an impression, you do not forget them for the rest of your life! But it all tasted twice as good because I was so relieved that our father was still alive.

The following day the solemn funeral of his brother took place. I celebrated the Mass for the Dead, although I had an uncle who was also a priest, but he was being a bit difficult. He kept saying that he was too old, he was sick, he was nervous, and therefore could I do it. Of course I agreed and then celebrated the Requiem Mass. Afterward, there was a large reception, too. I was glad that I went along with Father, because in that way I could become acquainted with his birthplace.

At the end of the summer semester in 1953, when he was recommended to take the chair of dogmatic and fundamental theology at the College of Philosophy and Theology in Freising, Joseph Ratzinger at first gratefully declined. He wanted to devote himself now entirely to his habilitation[3] *in Munich. His teacher and advisor was again Professor Gottlieb Söhngen, a lively theologian from Cologne who was the product of a "mixed marriage" and for that reason alone had an open mind for ecumenical questions, too. Söhngen had taught him how important it is to start with the sources themselves and to disregard later interpretations of them. Because Ratzinger had dealt in his dissertation with Augustine, the great Doctor of the Church in late antiquity, the professor suggested that he should now concentrate on a medieval Doctor of the Church; for instance, Saint Bonaventure (1217–1274), who is considered a great mystic and the most important theologian of the Franciscan Order. They quickly agreed on a topic: "Saint Bonaventure's Concept of Revelation and Theology of History".*

By the summer of 1954, Ratzinger had gathered the material for his habilitation *dissertation and worked out the main outline; now he still faced the difficult task of making a book out of it. In Freising, his plans were already set. The death of an emeritus professor of philosophy from*

---

[3] The *habilitation* is a second dissertation qualifying the candidate to hold a professorship at a German university.—TRANS.

the college had left a nice residence for a professor vacant, and as of the winter semester 1955–1956 he was supposed to take over the chair of fundamental theology. Until then the twenty-seven-year-old was already giving lectures in dogmatic theology as the acting chair.

At the end of the 1955 summer semester, the handwritten manuscript of his habilitation dissertation was finally finished. All he needed now was someone to type it for him. Yet the typist he found proved to be somewhat incompetent. She was slow, misplaced one sheet of paper or another, continually made mistakes, and mixed up the page references. Ratzinger was at his wit's end. His battle against the annoying typographical errors that spread like an epidemic and his desperate attempt to correct mistakes page by page exhausted him. Then in late autumn, he thought he had finally mastered the situation. Not exactly happy about its printed appearance, but convinced he had prevented the worst, he submitted the two obligatory copies of his habilitation dissertation to the theology faculty in Munich. He had done the work thoroughly and was sure he would qualify.

So he had his parents come to Freising, where they were to spend their twilight years. His father had just turned seventy-eight, his mother seventy-one, and, despite the idyllic setting, their life on the old farm outside Traunstein had become arduous. However attached the whole family was to the quiet house at the forest's edge, it was simply unsuitable as a senior citizens' residence. Joseph's new professorial residence, in contrast, was large enough for a whole family. It was located in a former manor of a cathedral canon, the so-called "Lerchenfeldhof" on the Domberg, right next to the church and quite close to the shops. His sister, Maria, was also thinking of joining the family household.

The move took place on a foggy day in November; the dreary atmosphere only intensified the sadness of his parents. For them a chapter of their life was coming to an end, which despite the horrors of the war had still been the best of their lives. They sensed that the time of their departure had now begun irrevocably. Nevertheless, they bravely tackled the new challenge. No sooner had the furniture movers arrived than Mother Ratzinger put on her apron to help. That evening she was

standing at the stove again preparing supper. Her husband meanwhile
was busy giving orders to the army of students who had come to help
them move in. Now they looked forward to being able to celebrate Christ-
mas again in their family circle.

At that time Joseph Ratzinger had no idea that storm clouds were
gathering. His teacher, Professor Söhngen, had already read his habil-
itation *dissertation and was so enthusiastic about it that he quoted it*
repeatedly in his lectures. In contrast, his colleague, Professor Schmaus,
who was the other reader and likewise had to approve it, took his time.
At some point in February of 1956 he began to read it. At Easter,
when he met Ratzinger at a congress of the Working Community of
German Dogmatists and Fundamental Theologians in Königstein, he
asked to talk with him for a moment. Briefly, to the point, and with no
emotion whatsoever, Schmaus informed him that he unfortunately had
to reject his habilitation.

Joseph Ratzinger was utterly crestfallen. His whole world seemed
suddenly to collapse. What was to become of him, what was to become
of his parents, whom he had in good faith just brought to live with him,
thinking they would be able to move into a professorial residence? As a
candidate who had failed to qualify, he would have to leave the college
like a beaten dog. In any case, he could still apply for a position as an
assistant pastor, which also came with a residence. But that prospect was
not especially comforting to him.

Later he learned the reason for Schmaus' negative attitude. First of
all, it was offended vanity. Medieval studies in Munich, of which he
was essentially the one proponent, had come to an almost complete
standstill in the prewar period. More recent findings, for instance, from
the French-speaking world, were ignored. The fact that Ratzinger crit-
icized certain positions with an acuity that was rather daring for a
beginner must not have sat well with Schmaus. He resented all the
more the fact that Ratzinger had worked on a medieval topic without
having entrusted himself to his direction. Then the inadequate printed
appearance and various errors in the references, which had remained
despite all the efforts during proofreading, served as a convenient excuse

for a devastating overall judgment. Schmaus considered Joseph Rat-
zinger a theological rebel who dared to take a stand against prevailing
scholarly opinion and thereby opened the door to a dangerous modern-
ism that would lead to a subjective concept of revelation. Rumors from
Freising about the refreshing modernity of Ratzinger's theology seemed
only to confirm this impression.

Yet although Schmaus was highly respected by his colleagues, he did
not succeed in winning over the faculty meeting to reject this habili-
tation dissertation entirely. The work was not rejected but only given
back to be revised. What needed revision was obvious from the mar-
ginal notes that Schmaus had written on his copy, which was now
presented to Ratzinger. The extent of the reworking that would be
required was so great that it would probably take years to do it, the
offended professor triumphantly remarked. Yet as Joseph worked through
the badly disfigured copy of his book, he noticed that all the criticism
referred only to his definition of the concept of revelation. The last
part, about Bonaventure's theology of history, had remained to a very
large extent uncontested. So an idea occurred to him that saved the
day: he would simply detach this part from the rest and concentrate
exclusively on that one theme. After some minor reworking, he was
able to submit the now abridged work as early as October 1956. On
February 11, 1957, he learned that this time his habilitation disser-
tation had been accepted. Nevertheless, he still had to give a public
habilitation lecture and defend it afterward—a requirement he could
likewise fail, and this time publicly. With considerable anxiety, Rat-
zinger prepared feverishly for that day, February 21. When the moment
finally came, the large auditorium that had been selected for the cer-
emony was bursting at the seams. A strange, almost palpable tension
was in the air. After his lecture, the reader, Professor Söhngen, and
the second reader, Professor Schmaus, took the floor. The two scholars
got into such a passionate debate that Ratzinger soon wondered whether
he was still needed there at all. The subsequent deliberation lasted a
long time. Finally, though, the dean came out into the corridor where
Joseph was waiting with his brother and several friends to tell him

quite unceremoniously that he had passed and thus qualified for a professorship.

He was now, at the age of twenty-nine, a professor, yet he could not really rejoice in the fact. The difficult path to this goal still hung over his head like a nightmare. Only gradually did the anxiety dissipate. Now he could continue his service in Freising in peace, without subjecting his parents to painful uncertainties. Despite the massive firepower deployed by Schmaus, he was finally appointed officially as extraordinary professor of fundamental and dogmatic theology at the College of Philosophy and Theology in Freising on January 1, 1958. The experience had taught him one thing, at least, that he took to heart again and again throughout his years as a professor. Whenever a dissertation or habilitation study was being debated and was in danger of being rejected, he sided with the weaker party whenever possible.

Actually I only learned later about the turbulent story surrounding my brother's *habilitation*. In 1955, I passed my exams at the music college and then completed the master class as well, for which there was no final examination. In 1957, I was supposed to complete my studies, and my brother only said that we would be done then at the same time: he with his *habilitation* and I with music college. The difficulties probably were due primarily to the competition between Professors Söhngen and Schmaus, since each of them wanted to be the better and more important scholar. As a result, he almost blocked my brother's *habilitation*. But I heard about all that only on the day when he was to defend his dissertation, for I had long since not been living in Munich; in late 1953, I had been transferred to Dorfen, at Ruprechtsberg, to Assumption parish with its impressive miraculous image of the Mother of God. I was choirmaster there at the same time—and therefore had to direct both parish choirs—and also curate for pilgrimages as well as a religion teacher and pastoral minister. So I did not have all that much time to follow developments in my brother's *habilitation*.

Yet of course I was there and helped energetically when he brought our parents to Freising. The two of us had deliberated about it for a long time and considered it the best solution. As I already told you, they lived at that time in an old farmhouse surrounded by as much land as could be worked in a day, which was being used for agriculture. As the years went by, it became too much work for our father. Then, too, it was over a mile to church, and you had to walk a distance to go shopping, and all that was rather tiresome for our parents. My brother's colleagues were urging him at the time to set up a household, and so we decided that if he had a residence, we would bring our parents, for in that case they could live with him from then on. When the time finally came, we sold their house in Traunstein. At that time I went back home again to help them pack. There is a photo that shows my parents and me standing for the last time in front of the house that had been our beloved home for so long (*see photo on page* 128). As you can imagine, the move was very difficult for our parents, especially for our father. He had grown up as a farm boy, and a farmer always takes a certain delight in his property, even though in this case it was only a small one, for he was actually a civil servant. But even so, it was difficult for him to part with it, although we sold the house at a good price to our neighbor.

Father and Mother then moved to Freising. They had some difficulties getting settled there, although from the start my brother made every effort to prepare a nice home for them. At first our sister remained in Traunstein, where she had an office job. Not until February of the following year did she give it up and move in also with my brother, so as to be able to care for our parents.

In every respect, they strove to support him in his work. In those days, my brother also had to administer examinations—there were many exams each semester—and he preferred to do that in his residence. So our father then invited the theologians in and led them into the living room where they could wait. Our mother brewed a cup of tea for each one and offered a few cookies with it, so that everything went smoothly and humanely. For our parents, in turn, it was good they had a task and could take care of these young gentlemen, future priests. Our father looked after them; our mother even cooked for them.

Once there was a young priest—my brother told me this story—who had already studied in Rome and was very gifted. He had written an interesting doctoral dissertation and frequently visited Joseph. So my brother told our parents that that priest could someday become Archbishop of Munich and Freising, he thought so much of him. Our parents welcomed him with the utmost reverence from then on, for they really thought he was the future archbishop. In reality, he later became, not the archbishop, but only the vicar general: I am talking about Gerhard Gruber (b. 1928). At first he became the secretary and advisor of Cardinal Döpfner at the Second Vatican Council, because he spoke perfect Italian, and then dean of the cathedral chapter and vicar general.

For two semesters Professor Ratzinger, as he was now called, remained in Freising. He was considered "the youngest theology professor in the world", and as a "theological wunderkind" he received offers from the most famous academic institutions. One of them came from Bonn, the destination of which his teacher Professor Söhngen had always dreamed and which eventually became Joseph's dream also. For a few weeks the young professor wavered about whether or not he should accept it. As far as his parents were concerned, he had soon found a solution for them. His brother Georg had completed his studies at the Munich College of Music in 1957 and was now supposed to return as choir director to his home parish of Saint Oswald in Traunstein. He would also take on the music director's duties at the minor seminary in Traunstein. A pretty little house in the middle of the city was assigned to him for his lodgings; it was big enough for three. Whereas it was unthinkable to take his aged parents with him to the city on the Rhine, a return to their beloved Traunstein seemed entirely feasible. Georg immediately agreed with this plan and urged his brother to accept the offer from Bonn. Then they spoke with their father, who did not find it altogether easy to accept but absolutely wanted his son to avail himself of this new opportunity. So the family parted ways. For the last time, Joseph had the privilege of sensing the security of being at home with his parents before a new adventure began. On April 15, 1959, he gave his inaugural lecture as a professor of fundamental theology at the University of Bonn. The topic was "The God of Faith and the God of Philosophy".

I still remember it well: at that time I was already living in Traunstein, when he visited me and told me he had received an invitation to teach in Bonn. What should he do now? How should he respond? After all, exactly one year before that he had brought our parents to Freising, and for that they had given up their property, their house in Traunstein. Then I said it was no problem, since I was living all alone in a benefice house in Traunstein that was big enough for all of us. I had to start a household anyway, and so I would be happy to have them move in with me: "They know Traunstein, and so they will be happy to come back. Take this opportunity. You must not let it pass you by: take it! Our parents will come stay with me; I look forward to having them come." With that, the matter was settled for both of us; now he just had to convince our parents, too. He then moved in April 1959. Maria went with him to keep house for him in Bonn, while our parents came to live with me in May.

Joseph Ratzinger loved the Rhineland, its openness and tolerance. Whereas Bavaria was rather conservative and had a rural character, here one sensed how the river united nations and cultures, mutually enriching them. His first semester in the Rhineland university city was for him like "an

ongoing honeymoon" with "wonderful memories" (M 118). But soon
the cheerfulness of the new beginning was overshadowed.

Christmas of 1958 was once again an especially harmonious celebration. Our father gave expensive presents to all of us—to each one of us, to the extent his means allowed. Of course, we did not yet suspect that this would be our last Christmas together.

After their move, my brother and our sister spent their vacation in Traunstein, and it was a magnificent summer, that August of 1959. Eight days before Father's death, Mother came to me one night and said that Father was sick, and would I look in on him. I then went downstairs to their room and gave him a few drops of Karmelitergeist,[4] which did him some good. We also called a doctor, who could not find any cause for concern. On the day when he finally suffered a stroke, he was actually quite himself. That morning he walked up to the seminary, which was a distance of over a mile, because my brother was preaching there. In the afternoon, he took a long walk with our mother—one that I at that age would not have been able to manage at all. Later Mother told us how they went by the parish church on their way back. They went in, and Father prayed with special intensity. Actually, he was always someone who prayed devoutly, yet she noticed then a particular fervor about his prayer that for us was a sign he must have sensed already that death was drawing near. That same evening, then, he had the stroke and lost consciousness and collapsed as though dead.

We three siblings had traveled that day to Tittmoning and toured the city of our childhood. It was a wonderful excursion; we were quite happy and had no idea that the end of the day would be so sad and upsetting. Two days later, on August 25, 1959, our father died as a result of that stroke.

---

[4] "Carmelite spirits" is an herbal remedy.—TRANS.

For us it was a crushing blow. Of course then the four of us dealt with all the formalities; there are always so many technical things to do when someone you love has died that at first they keep you from surrendering to your feelings. He left us so quickly, so unexpectedly, and suddenly our life together as a family was over. It had begun with the birth of my brother, which brought us to our full number, and lasted until that August day in the year 1959. After that, a pillar was missing from our family life. Someone who had always belonged to it, indeed, who was the head of that family, was no longer there. Yet as sad as we were, we knew, on the other hand, that he had died a good death, which in such cases is always a consolation. He did not suffer; everything happened very quickly. And at least we all had the opportunity to be present at his death and to say goodbye. Above all, though, we knew and trusted that although Father was in another world, he was still with us somehow and united with us.

The fact that Joseph Ratzinger had accepted the invitation to go to Bonn proved in retrospect to be one of the most important decisions of his life—and really a providential act. There he met a man who was to become for him a new father figure—and who ultimately opened for him the doors leading to Rome.

Joseph Cardinal Frings, Archbishop of Cologne, was the most impressive and most influential personage in the German episcopate during the postwar period. His mixture of warm humor, roots in the Rhineland, deep faith, and wisdom was legendary. From the very beginning, the tall, gaunt son of a manufacturer from Neuss, who inscribed the motto "Appointed for the People" on his episcopal coat of arms, was beloved by believing Catholics. In 1946, when Pope Pius XII conferred the rank of cardinal upon him and two other German bishops—Konrad Graf von Preysing and Clemens Graf von Galen, who had distinguished themselves by their extraordinary resistance to the Brownshirt regime—this was considered a special sign of confidence in the German Church. From 1945 to 1965, Frings was president of the conference of German bishops. He preached an unforgettable sermon on New Year's Eve 1946, in which he referred to the looting of coal trains during a particularly harsh winter: "We are living in times where the individual in need ought to be allowed to take what he needs to preserve his life and health if he cannot obtain it in some other way, by working or asking for it." From then on, at least in the Cologne region, the verb "to frings" [fringsen] became the popular term for the "procurement" of food and pressed coal.

When he and the other cardinals elected John XXIII the new pope in 1958, he remarked in passing that he "had the feeling that now a general council should take place soon". Almost one hundred years had passed since the First Vatican Council, and so Frings believed that it was once again time to listen to the bishops. The new pope enthusiastically adopted the idea, announced a general council, and appointed Frings to the preparatory commission.

We all held Pope Pius XII in very, very high esteem, for everyone knew he had not only a great mind but also spiritual greatness. In those days, there were no anti-papal impulses; he was simply revered; he was our pope. Naturally, we were happy and a little bit proud to have an extraordinarily gifted pope of that caliber. But we also knew he was an old man who already suffered from various health problems. It was rumored that he had allowed a doctor to inject him with fresh cells so that he could remain healthy and active as long as possible, but, nevertheless, we were not all that surprised in October 1958 to learn of his death, as much as we regretted the loss.

His successor, John XXIII, was so different that you had to get used to it at first. He lacked the saintly majesty of a Pius XII, yet instead he radiated humanity all the more. He was a pope of the people, whom everybody actually liked; even Protestants raved about him.

In 1961, the Catholic Academy in Bensberg invited the "theological wunderkind" Ratzinger to share his thoughts about "the theology of

Conciliar theologian Professor Joseph Ratzinger (right) with the Archbishop of Cologne, Joseph Cardinal Frings

the Council". Cardinal Frings made a special trip from Cologne to listen to the comments. Through his secretary, Doctor Luthe, who had studied theology with Ratzinger in Munich, he had become aware of the Bavarian priest. When Ratzinger had finished, the Cardinal invited him to have a conversation. He told him that he had rather carelessly accepted an invitation to give a lecture in Genoa that was supposed to be about "the Council against the background of the current situation in contrast to the First Vatican Council". Meanwhile, he was seventy-four years old, almost blind, and therefore simply in physical terms no longer capable of completing such a demanding task. Could he help him with it? The young doctor of theology gladly consented.

The outline he submitted shortly thereafter was so good that Frings had to correct it at only one point. The speech itself was impressive and became the theological clarion call; it seemed as if the Cardinal had announced the theological program for the whole Council. Shortly thereafter, Frings was invited to a private audience with John XXIII, who greeted him enthusiastically: "Last night I read your lecture in Genoa and wanted to express my thanks to you." When the Cardinal pointed out to him that the lecture was not by him but by a certain Joseph Ratzinger, the Pope dismissed the remark. He, too, had to let others draft documents for him; hence the only thing that mattered was finding the right advisors. From that moment on, it was clear that Ratzinger would continue to be Frings' collaborator, the "best horse in his stable", so to speak. The Cardinal, though, was appointed by the Pope to be one of a ten-member central preparatory commission for the Council. As such, he received copies of all the drafts and suggestions that were composed by the individual commissions in advance and were to be presented to the bishops at the Council for a vote. One after the other, he presented them to Ratzinger for his expert opinion.

Then the great day came. On October 11, 1962, with a solemn Mass in Saint Peter's Basilica, Pope John XXIII opened the Second Vatican Council, at which 2,800 bishops from all parts of the world were to shape the future of the Church. Cardinal Frings had not traveled to it alone. He was accompanied by the thirty-five-year-old Joseph Ratzinger, who had now officially become his theological advisor. It was the latter's first experience with the universal Church—and his great opportunity to help shape her future. Here Ratzinger became acquainted with some of the most important theologians of his time—Henri de Lubac, Jean Daniélou, Yves Congar, Gérard Philips. At the end of the first session, he was even appointed an official conciliar theologian, a peritus. Even before the Council started, he had lamented the fact that the Church had "reins that are too tight, too many laws, many of which have helped to leave the century of unbelief in the lurch, instead of helping it to redemption" (SE 73). Now it was time to make a leap forward and to dare to try something new. Faith, Ratzinger said, must "get out of its armor; it also had to face the situation of the present in a new language, in new openness. So a greater freedom also had to arise in the Church" (SE 73).

Cardinal Frings planned to exert his influence at the Council with almost military precision. At his initiative, all the German and Austrian bishops met every Monday at 5:00 P.M. in the seminary of Santa

*Maria dell'Anima near the Piazza Navona to discuss the course of the
Council and its results. Skilled theologians, including Ratzinger, regularly commented on the events and developed strategies. Although it was
a small group, it was extremely influential. Frings himself was one of
the most respected personages in the Catholic world. As co-founder of
the bishops' charitable organization Misereor, he was very popular, especially among the bishops from the Third World. Thus his circle managed to write conciliar history.*

In 1962, my brother and I traveled for the first time together to
Rome. I still recall that we rode the "Rapidissimo", the supposedly high-speed train, and marveled at its name, which it did
not deserve at all since it stopped at practically every station. Of
course then we went sight-seeing and visited the most famous
churches, Saint Peter's Basilica, for example, and Santa Maria
Maggiore, and were profoundly impressed by the Eternal City.

Later, Joseph used to tell stories about the Council. I think it
was 1964 when the dean of Traunstein was able to persuade him
to give a lecture at the seminary for the clergy of the deanery
and to give an eyewitness report, so to speak, on the events and
discussions in Rome. The whole seminary was full, and the court-
yard was full of automobiles, because all the priests from the
entire region had come to hear my brother's lecture about the
Council. I knew most of what he talked about already from
private conversations, but the lecture was very appealing and led
to an animated discussion afterward. Above all, he emphasized
at that time the great vivacity at the Council and the fact that
even in clerical circles there was a certain lack of unity, that
there were different opinions about clerical matters and articles
of our faith, about which people were having free and open
discussion—and he was very pleased with that.

*Very soon it became clear that the Council in Rome had been a cause
not only of joy. Whereas the Pope spoke about "aggiornamento",*

bringing the Church up-to-date, conservative churchmen feared too many innovations. Their spokesman was Alfredo Cardinal Ottaviani, the Prefect of the Holy Office, the dicastery that succeeded the infamous Roman Inquisition. As president of the theological commission, he did everything he could to impede reforms.

In June 1963, Pope John XXIII succumbed to cancer. The Council, which had only just begun, seemed to have run aground. Yet against all opposition, the new pope, Paul VI, continued it. Finally, when it became known that Ottaviani's commission intended to declare a vote by the bishops invalid "because the questions were inadequately framed", Frings ran out of patience. In what was perhaps the most sensational speech of the whole Council, he not only criticized the subterfuges of the prefect, but also directly attacked his Office and described it as a "stumbling block": its method of condemning people without giving them a hearing no longer suited today's world. Although Ottaviani venomously retorted that Frings obviously knew nothing about the work of the Holy Office, he had nevertheless lost that battle. The bishops were on the side of the prelate from Cologne, and their thunderous applause vindicated him. On that same day, the Pope summoned Frings, who had to fear the worst. He drily noted in the Cologne dialect to his secretary, Doctor Luthe: "Hängen Se m'r noch ens dat ruude Mäntelche öm, wer weiss, ob et nit et letzte Mohl is." (Put that little red robe on me once again; who knows, it might be the last time.) Yet as he entered the audience chamber, the Pope hurried over to him and embraced him: "Dear Cardinal, you said everything that I thought and wanted to say but could not say myself." When the Council ended in 1965, Paul VI declared that the Holy Office was deprived of its authority. It would now be replaced by the "Congregation for the Doctrine of the Faith" and was to lose its status as an absolute authority. The new dicastery applied democratic principles for the first time. It did not condemn; it issued warnings and invited troublesome theologians to a dialogue. The Vatican had entered the modern era.

During the time of the Council, however, what was perhaps the most profound upheaval in the life of the Ratzinger brothers also occurred:

*the death of their beloved mother a week before Christmas, on Decem-
ber 16, 1963.*

Our mother had already had stomach problems for a long time.
It actually began in March 1963, when she often complained
about stomach pains. She used to say then that "Italian food"
was best for her, but that was a Tyrolean expression equiva-
lent to "go hungry and eat nothing", because under Italian
rule the inhabitants of Tyrol were not so well off. She recovered shortly, but then it became even worse, and she had to
vomit repeatedly.

In August, my brother and I traveled to Lienz in East Tyrol
and spent our vacation there in the Wiener Sängerknaben (Vienna
Boys' Choir) hotel. At that time she had made an appointment
at the hospital to have a stomach X-ray. She traveled there with
our sister, underwent the examination, and the doctor's fears were
confirmed: it was stomach cancer.

Despite the diagnosis, she continued to keep house for me,
while my brother had to go to Rome again. That summer he
moved from Bonn to Münster, where he had accepted a new
professorship, and Maria had plenty to do setting up a new household for him there. Later on she did come join us to take care
of our mother.

*In the summer of 1963, Professor Joseph Ratzinger left his beloved
Bonn. Hermann Volk, a dogmatic theologian in Münster, had become
the bishop of Mainz in the summer of 1962, and now his professorial
chair was vacant. Volk himself had requested Ratzinger as his successor,
but he refused at first. Only when two young students were in danger
of having their doctoral dissertations rejected because of opposition by his
colleagues did he see it as destiny beckoning. In Münster, he knew, he
would be able to help the two students more. So finally he moved to the
university city in Westphalia and took his two doctoral candidates right
with him; eventually they succeeded in earning their degrees.*

At that time our mother had already become bedridden; she was vomiting regularly and suffering horribly. It was a difficult time for us. She became thinner and thinner, was able to eat less and less, and was actually afraid to take any food, because she did not know whether she would be able to keep it down. In early December, I finally wrote to my brother that she was in a bad way, and he came immediately. We spent the last two weeks together, my siblings, my mother, and I. It was terrible to watch how she kept fading, until it was plain that she was gradually dying. We then called the pastor, who heard her confession and gave her extreme unction, while she was quite weak and subdued. To the end she carried the burden of her life patiently, with the strength of her faith; she was like a candle that is increasingly consumed and yet radiates its light.

"Her goodness became even purer and more radiant and continued to shine unchanged even through the weeks of increasing pain. . . . I know of no more convincing proof for the faith than precisely the pure and unalloyed humanity that the faith allowed to mature in my parents and in so many other persons I have had the privilege to encounter", Joseph Ratzinger wrote in his memoirs (M 131).

When my brother was born in Marktl, the *bader* (barber-surgeon) pulled our mother's teeth, because they were all decayed and some were festering at the roots, and made a denture for her. That denture, made by a simple barber-surgeon, held up wonderfully until the 1960s without any part of it breaking off. But then, when she was getting thinner and thinner, it was suddenly too big. For us, that was an upsetting sign: Mother's teeth no longer fit because she was losing so much weight.

She died around noon on a rather cold day. So we had to reopen the grave in which we had buried our father four years earlier. Eight days later, it was Christmas. It was the saddest and most lonely Christmas of our whole life.

GEDENKET IM GEBET

meines lieben Gatten, unseres guten Vaters

Herrn Joseph Ratzinger

Gendarmeriemeister i. R.

geb. am 6. März 1877 in Rieckering
bei Schwanenkirchen/Niederbayern
gest. am 25. August 1959 in Traunstein

Deinen Gläubigen, o Herr, wird das Leben nicht
genommen, es wird nur neu gestaltet. Wenn diese
Herberge ihres Erdenwandelns in Staub zerfällt,
steht ihnen eine ewige Heimat im Himmel bereit.
(Aus der Totenliturgie der Kirche.)

Chiemgau-Druck, Traunstein

Gedenket im Gebet
unserer lieben, guten Mutter

Frau Maria Ratzinger

Gendarmeriemeisterswitwe

geb. am 8. Jan. 1884 in Mühlbach
gest. am 16. Dez. 1963 in Traunstein

Auf Dich, o Herr, habe ich gehofft.
Ich werde nicht zuschanden in Ewigkeit.
(Ambrosianischer Lobgesang)

Chiemgau-Druck, Traunstein

Commemorative prayer cards for the pope's parents, Joseph (d. 1959) and Maria (d. 1963) Ratzinger

My brother "inherited" a lot from our mother. Like her, he is very tenderhearted; he loves animals and flowers. I can remember how he as a little boy once sat in a meadow for hours and picked flowers. He got that from our mother, and from our father somehow his rational side. These two qualities of our parents combined in him in a special way.

At the time when our mother became sick, negotiations were already in progress for my transfer to Regensburg. Mother was still able to hear the news and was happy about it.

The long-time director of the Regensburg Domspatzen, cathedral choirmaster Doctor Theobald Shrems, was suffering then from a malignant form of cancer, and shortly before his seventieth birthday he was looking for a suitable successor. It had to be a cleric who had already made a public appearance as a gifted musician and choir director. At some point,

his former piano teacher at the Munich Music College, Professor Fritz
Hübsch, told him about Georg Ratzinger, who at that time had already
made a name for himself as a choir director in Traunstein. After making
initial contact with him in early 1963, Schrems recommended him as
his favorite candidate to succeed him in the position. Immediately after
his death on November 15, 1963, the negotiations began.

If our mother had survived, I would not have gone to Regensburg, for I could not have asked her to make the move. Yet our
idyllic life in Traunstein did end then. I was living there in a
beautiful house connected with a benefice, the so-called "little
preacher's house", in which our parents had felt so much at home.
Mother had her little garden where she could work, which she
always liked to do. Yet when she had died, all that ceased to
have any value for me, and so I left Traunstein and went to
Regensburg. It was the biggest upheaval in my life. My siblings
of course still visited me in Regensburg and had their room with
the Domspatzen (*that is, at the* gymnasium *of the Regensburg Dom-*
spatzen, which was nicknamed the "Kaff"). It was always quite nice
there, yet it was also a totally different world, to which we first
had to become accustomed.

    For me, the first years in Regensburg were rather difficult. At
that time, the two nephews of my predecessor were still active
in the house of the Domspatzen. One of them, Hans Schrems,
had acted on behalf of his uncle for a long time and recently,
when the latter was sick, had even conducted the main choir.
The other, Fritz Schrems, was responsible for the finances. Both
of them gave me the feeling that I was somehow unwelcome,
like a fifth wheel on a wagon. Several years went by before this
changed. Hans Schrems, the choir director, met a tragic end; on
November 7, 1969, he was found dead beneath the bridge over
the Danube in Regensburg. Yet as sad as that was, at least it
ended the established regime that had oppressed me personally
and artistically, while I lacked the energy to offer resistance to it.

Only from that point on was I the "master of the house", who also, in practice, conducted the Regensburg Domspaten choir.

Not only artistically, but also personally everything was now "in tune" again with the world-famous boys choir. The "Chief", as they called Georg Ratzinger, quickly succeeded in winning the hearts of the boys who sang in it. His phenomenal memory enabled him to learn the names and stories of the youngsters quickly, so that even the new students were surprised that he already knew so much about them. Since the nuns in the house of the Domspatzen provided him super-abundantly with pretzels, candy, and cake, he invited the choir boys every day at 4:00 in the afternoon to his legendary "Raubtierfütterung" (feeding time for the beasts of prey), which soon became a fixture in the daily routine, an opportunity that many of them continued to take even long after their careers as choristers were over. Yet as kindly as he was toward the boys during free time, there was just as much discipline during choir practices. Georg Ratzinger hated a lack of punctuality and demanded the highest level of achievement. Only in that way did he succeed in forming the boys choir of the cathedral city into a world-famous institution, which not only toured all of Europe in the "Kaff-bomber"—the aging tour bus of the Domspatzen—but at the same time went on tour twice each in the United States (1983 and 1987) and in Japan (1988 and 1991). Yet the high point in the history of the choir was first of all another tour: in October 1965, the Domspatzen appeared in Rome and sang for the Council Fathers and Pope Paul VI. His brother, Joseph, had arranged that great event.

The performance in Rome was of course a thoroughly wonderful experience and the high point of my career as cathedral choirmaster. At that point in time, I had been in Regensburg for less than two years; my predecessor's nephews and the whole group that had flocked around them were still there, but I was the choir director, in any case. Our first concert for the Council

Fathers took place in the great hall of the Angelicum, the college of the Dominicans. Then we had the privilege of singing at a conciliar Mass at Saint Peter's. The whole basilica was filled with two thousand bishops from all over the world, along with the Council observers, and at the end the Council Secretary, Archbishop Pericle Felici, said, "Optime, sed nunc exite!" (Excellent, but now out with you!) In addition, we sang a beautiful liturgy in the German national church in Rome, Santa Maria dell'Anima; it was a major feast day, too. And finally we made another appearance at an audience Pope Paul VI gave for the Catholic Academy in Bavaria and for us, too. It was a special audience for this limited group and naturally a great experience for the boys, and for me in any case, that they were able to sing there in front of the Pope.

We gave another special concert for the Catholic Academy in a room that Raphael had decorated, in the Villa Farnesina, a wonderful Roman *palazzo*. It was all like a dream, and the boys were overjoyed to be able to experience Rome and the events of the Council. We traveled by train and stayed in the Kolping House; that was certainly nice. I still remember one detail about the return trip as though it were yesterday. I went to the boys when I heard that Haller was there. Helmut Haller (*b. 1939*) was at that time a famous player on the German national soccer team. And so many of them went to him and asked for an autograph. But that of course was an incidental experience; the decisive thing for us all was the stay in Rome. I think we were well received everywhere. Wherever we went, people were enthusiastic about our singing. That gave us a lot of encouragement and self-confidence, making appearances abroad now as a choir and from then on practically traveling around the world.

Of course the reform of the liturgy that followed the Second Vatican Council was a considerable adjustment for us at first. I must confess that by nature I am someone who is oriented to custom and does not surrender it thoughtlessly. I will be the first to admit that it is a bit difficult for me to learn completely new things and to put them into practice. Our bishop at the time, Rudolf Graber (*1903–1992*), was very understanding, and the whole cathedral chapter was also. To a large extent, we still cultivated the old liturgy. The Regensburg tradition had already existed before, and my predecessor raised awareness of it even more, so that it was viewed as an obligation to continue it and to keep singing the way it had always been done, even though all around us things had long since changed. Besides, valuable things that were once considered important and were well received should not be given away, either, without further ado. So we were not only permitted to keep practicing the old music, but it was considered our duty. New elements were added only step by step. That way it was not a painful break but, rather, a gradual and somewhat organic development over the years, so as to loosen up more and more the liturgy from those days, which was, after all, a bit rigid.

While my brother was teaching in Bonn, first, and then in Münster, I often visited him and my sister there and spent my vacation with them both. I also used the time to attend lectures at the University of Bonn and later in Münster and Tübingen. I simply looked in the course catalogue for sessions that interested me, both in musicology and in theology. I liked Bonn very much; I felt very much at ease in that beautiful city. Most importantly, Professor Johann Auer (*1910–1989*) was there, too, whom I knew from Freising, where he was our professor for dogmatic theology. He was a native of Regensburg, actually a simple man who in his free time spoke the thickest Bavarian dialect, and we always got along wonderfully.

Naturally my brother missed his Bavarian homeland even then. The presence of other Bavarians, though, such as Professor Auer and another one, the medievalist Professor Ludwig Hödl (*b. 1924*), who was in my class, gave him the feeling that he was not all that much of a stranger in Bonn. In Münster, too, he adjusted quickly. That was also a very beautiful city, well tended and clean; there was really no reason to complain, yet the longing for Bavaria was still there. Our sister, too, dreamed about returning to our homeland, which perhaps influenced him a little. Love of homeland is very often greater among us Bavarians than among North Germans.

So the temptation was irresistible when the University of Tübingen offered him in 1966 a newly created chair in dogmatic theology. One theologian in Tübingen who had strongly advocated recruiting Ratzinger was Hans Küng. The two men met in 1957 at a congress of dogmatic theologians in Innsbruck (see M 135)—only later would they become opponents.

His students in Münster had very positive memories of Ratzinger. When the newspaper Die Rheinische Post *asked several of them in April 2005, their impression was always the same. They described him as a reserved, amiable man who not only could think analytically but also radiated much warmth and humanity. Pastor Fritz Lemming, for instance, who at that time was an instructor in dogmatic theology, recalled: "He was the kindliest of all examiners. When the other professors noticed that a candidate was well acquainted with a field, they changed the subject. Ratzinger, in contrast, stayed at every oasis of knowledge he discovered." At that time, he was living in a little house on the Aasee [a lake]. He rode to his lectures on an old bicycle that his students had bought for him at an auction. Since he had no driver's license, they often drove him home again after the lecture. Often he invited his students to his house for a meal. In a circle of close acquaintances, he then thawed and told anecdotes and jokes by Karl Valentin.*[5]

Then when the call to Tübingen came, he told me that that was closer to Bavaria. A train ride to Münster, after all, was rather tiresome; it took a long time to travel in those days.

---

[5] Karl Valentin was a Bavarian comedian, the "Charlie Chaplin of Germany".—TRANS.

However promising the changes in the Church after the Council were, they were fundamentally misunderstood by many people. Thus Ratzinger, as one of the co-authors of the document Lumen gentium *(Light of the nations), helped establish the practice of defining the Church, as New Israel, as "People of God" that live from the Body of Christ, the Eucharist, and so herself becomes the Body of Christ. What this meant was that the Church should unite herself more closely to Jesus, who in calling his apostles was concerned about sending a "new people" on its way. The concept "People of God" became connected with such exciting and questionable things as the increased importance of the laity in the Church, the notion of the autonomy of the episcopal office and of episcopal collegiality as opposed to papal primacy, a greater importance of local Churches vis-à-vis Rome, and a broadening of the concept of Church in ecumenical terms.*

After the Council, the expression was taken up enthusiastically, but in a way that neither Ratzinger nor the Council Fathers had intended. Suddenly it became a slogan: "We are the People!" The idea of a "Church from below" developed; its proponents wanted to engage in polemics against those who held office and to carry out their agenda by democratic majority vote. Although the theological, biblical concept of people was still the idea of a natural hierarchy, of a great family, suddenly it was reinterpreted in a Marxist sense, in which "people" is always considered the antithesis to the ruling classes. The center of the Christian faith, however, can only be God's revelation, which cannot be put to a ballot. Church is being called by God. Joseph Ratzinger said: "The crisis concerning the Church, as it is reflected in the crisis concerning the concept 'People of God', is a 'crisis about God': it is the result of leaving out what is most essential. What then remains is merely a dispute about power. There is already enough of that elsewhere in the world—we do not need the Church for that" (PF 129). The Council Fathers had appeared in Rome so as to bring the faith with its full impact into the present day. But many understood "reform" to mean, not renewing, but watering down the faith. Their spokesman was the same Hans Küng who had just brought Ratzinger along to Tübingen, probably because he saw him as another reformer.

And so in the Swabian university city, two men who could not have been more different collided. While Hans Küng drove around in his Alfa Romeo, Joseph Ratzinger rode to lectures on his rusty bike. While the flamboyant, highly vocal Küng rose to the position of figurehead of the progressives, Ratzinger at first offered quiet resistance. Anyone who maintains that in Tübingen he switched over to the conservative camp has thoroughly misunderstood him. He only remained true to himself and did not turn like a weathervane with every breeze of the spirit of the age.

The conflict took place against the backdrop of the *1968* rebellions. The student movement wanted to drive "the mustiness of a thousand years" (IP *201*) out of the university gowns. The generation of their parents was accused of complicity with the Nazi terror and slaughter of the Jews, of giving themselves absolution, and of bourgeois narrow-mindedness. They dreamed of free love and autonomy, new music and new values. Whereas the Western world defined itself at that time by its opposition to Communism, the generation of revolutionaries flirted with Marx. Marxism became the new doctrine of salvation that dispenses with God and replaces him with man's political action. Christ did not bring redemption; it must be won first in the world revolution! Thus it was clear that Marxism and Christianity were fundamentally irreconcilable. Yet despite this, there were "progressive" theologians who attempted precisely this balancing act without noticing they had long since left the firm ground of faith.

Even in Tübingen, Joseph Ratzinger never had trouble with his students; his lectures as always were crowded to overflowing. Yet when in theological circles some flyers began making the rounds that described the Cross as an "expression of a sado-masochistic glorification of pain" (SE *77*) under the slogan, "Cursed be Jesus!", he could no longer remain silent. It would have seemed to him a betrayal had he withdrawn into the peace and quiet of the lecture hall. During the Third Reich he had observed that political doctrines of self-redemption lead to ruin. While at first he still had some understanding "for the protest against a pragmatism born of material prosperity" (ST *62*), this tolerance ended when

violence and psychological terror began. Later he recalled: "In those years
I learned when a discussion must stop because it is turning into a lie
and when resistance is necessary in order to preserve freedom" (SE 76).
Together with Evangelical Lutheran theologians, he founded an action
league in order to prevent the faculty from being ruined by the Marxists.

Yet he had something to offer them as an alternative. In a series of lec-
tures that later appeared as a book entitled Introduction to Christianity *and became a bestseller in seventeen countries, he extolled the "beauty*
of the faith". The singular clarity and stylistic elegance with which he did
so soon earned him the reputation of being a "Mozart of theology". Upon
reading it, Karol Wojtyla, Archbishop of Krakow, believed he had found
a spiritual brother. Paul VI, too, was enthusiastic when the Italian edi-
tion was published. At his personal request, Ratzinger was appointed to
the International Theological Commission in 1969.

Tübingen was by no means a turning point in my brother's
thought but, rather, a time in which many things in his theological research were clarified and systematized. What he had
done and taught before was completed here, so to speak.

What had changed radically, though, were the surroundings
in which he worked. The year 1968 was like a bout of fever that
raged over Germany and the world. This 1968 environment was
politically determined and more influenced by political factors:
it wanted to politicize everything, even theology. Oddly enough,
many theologians caught the fever, the Lutherans much more
than we Catholics. In doing so, they themselves often did not
understand the wave in which they were caught up. They simply thought they had recognized something and did not realize
they had become victims of a momentary confusion that then
subsided again just as quickly. I noticed this even with the Domspatzen, among the men's voices. The older ones had suddenly
become more rebellious that year, whereas a year later they were
again quite well behaved and much simpler. At that time a spiritual wave came over us that was really irrational.

My brother certainly suffered from it somewhat. At that time his book *Introduction to Christianity* was published, and he then gave it to his students to read. It put many of them back on the right track. When they read it correctly and really took it to heart, it freed them from their unrealistic reveries and brought them back to the reality and rightness of the faith.

Actually, though, he felt quite happy in Tübingen. He had a nice house there and an itinerant cat that always visited him. It belonged to a noblewoman from the neighborhood. When she was nearby, the cat always acted as if it did not recognize my brother at all. Yet it came to visit him every day and was fed by him. It even accompanied him to his lectures and to Mass. It was a black cat, a very intelligent pussycat. Once a man on the street spoke to him and asked him how he had managed it, how he had trained the cat so well that it walked beside him. The man said that he had a little cat, too, that was dear to him, but it never wanted to come along when he went somewhere.

Tübingen, then, most certainly had its nice features. But then as things worked out, Regensburg got a university of its own and Joseph was to return to Bavaria. At first he belonged to the committee for academic appointments, as they were hiring the faculty of theology. At that time, he recommended Professor Auer from Bonn for the chair of dogmatic theology. Only when they created a second professorship in dogmatics was he finally willing to consent and come to Regensburg himself. And I was happy that our family was together again!

Although, technically speaking, this was a step backward in his career—Tübingen had the most renowned chair of theology in the republic, while Regensburg was considered the most obscure province—and it elicited sardonic comments from his colleagues, that did not matter to Joseph. He wanted finally to pursue his theological research again in peace and could not bear the grueling conflicts with his "progressive" colleagues.

In November 1969, then, he moved. A moving van brought most of his things, while his assistant, who was originally from Bierbronnen in the Black Forest, drove him and our sister to Regensburg. Of course a few things were packed in the car, too. Now it was an ancient automobile and no longer capable at all of being loaded down so heavily. When the rattletrap finally reached Regensburg, it was stopped right at the city limits by a policeman. He of course demanded to see the driver's license and the vehicle registration, but when he read where the car came from, he had to smirk. "You come from Bierbronnen; well, then just drive on", was all he said. He found it tremendously impressive that someone came from a locality with the beautiful name Bierbronnen (Beer springs).

My brother felt at home in Regensburg from the very beginning. A rather familiar atmosphere prevailed among the faculty; he got along well with his colleagues right away. At first he lived in a rented apartment. But then one of the cathedral canons helped him find a property in Pentling, a town near the university campus where several professors already lived. There he intended to build a house that eventually was to become the new center of our family. He really was looking forward to it. Every morning when he went to the church to celebrate Mass, he had to go by that plot of land. On the way home, he always used to imagine that next winter on that spot would stand his nicely heated house, while at the time the ground was still covered with a deep layer of snow. And that is exactly what happened, too. He had a very good architect, Herr Hans Scheininger, who spent most of his time on building projects in Mallersdorf and gave us many good suggestions. So he himself did not have to worry much about it while his house was being built according to his taste and his needs. Yet even when the house was completed, my brother always came first to my place on Sundays to have a midday meal together at the refectory of the Domspatzen. Only then did I ride with him out to Pentling, where we drank coffee together with our sister and spent a pleasant evening. There we could converse and relax. Finally, when we parted later in the evening, we already looked forward to the next Sunday, when we would meet again. So the house was for me also a place of refuge, a place where I knew I was always welcome. Of course both of us had a very full week; I was busy with the boys' choir, and he was often on lecture tours, while Maria kept the house, but he usually took weekends off for our family gathering.

He also made an effort to keep in close contact with the Domspatzen. On Christmas Eve, for instance, we had Vespers in the afternoon, followed by a nap for the youngsters, then the evening meal, and afterward the exchange of presents, and he always came to it. Before the dining hall, there was a small auditorium in which our Christmas celebration took place. First there was singing, then the Gospel was read aloud, I gave a little talk, and a few more Christmas carols were sung, and afterward the boys were allowed to go back into the dining room, where they received their presents. These were gifts that cost around twenty or thirty marks, and there was always a terrific din. As was formerly the custom in our family, punch was then served to the older boys. There was always a wonderful atmosphere before we went to the cathedral for midnight Mass.

When the sisters had to give up their kitchen duties, simply because there were too few of them, we hired a cook. He, however, did not know that the Domspatzen were only supposed to get a punch made with a few drops of alcohol and served instead quite an ordinary punch. Afterward, the younger boys were completely befuddled and no longer sang beautifully but just yelled. The next time, fortunately, the cook knew better.

In those days, we really thought that Regensburg was the last stop on my brother's itinerary. So we said to each other one day that our parents' grave was so lonely in Traunstein:

let's bring it now to Regensburg! In 1974, we had the tombstone and their earthly remains transported and buried them in the cemetery in Ziegetsdorf. But then once again everything turned out quite differently.

1. Habemus Papam! *Pope Benedict XVI appears and greets the faithful for the first time after his election*

2. *With the Domspatzen in the Sistine Chapel: Pope Benedict XVI thanks his brother, Msgr. Georg Ratzinger*

3. 1980: Cardinal J. Ratzinger introduces his brother to Pope John Paul II during a concert in Munich

4. The Ratzinger siblings in 1989 at the celebration of Georg Ratzinger's 65th birthday

5. 1999: The brothers during a visit to Prague

6-8. Devoted to Mary and his homeland: Pope Benedict XVI prays on September 11, 2006, in the Chapel of Graces in Altötting, and then he donates his episcopal ring to our Lady

9. On September 13, 2006, on the way to the "Old Chapel": Georg Ratzinger, Pope Benedict XVI, and the Bishop of Regensburg, Gerhard Ludwig Müller. In the background the house belonging to the Pope's brother

10. Pope Benedict XVI and his brother in Marktl am Inn, visiting the baptismal font over which Joseph Ratzinger was received into the communion of the Church on April 16, 1927

11. *A heartfelt desire: reconciliation with the Jews. Benedict XVI on May 11, 2009, in the Holocaust Memorial Yad Vashem*

12. *Good neighbors: meeting with Hans Rosengold, the head of the Jewish congregation in Regensburg*

13. *Msgr. Georg Ratzinger and Pope Benedict XVI at the grave of their parents in the cemetery in Ziegetsdorf*

14. *The Pope and his brother on vacation together*

15. *Georg Ratzinger is made an honorary citizen of the city Castel Gandolfo. His brother, the Pope, gives the eulogy*

16. *Relaxing at the piano: Benedict XVI on vacation*

17. *The Pope at work: Benedict XVI at his desk*

VIII

Cardinal

(1977–2005)

*I*n early 1977 this apparent security in the life of Professor Joseph Ratzinger ended again. One day when the papal nuncio Guido Del Mestri visited him on some pretense, he at first thought nothing of it. But after chatting about unimportant things, the Italian pulled a letter out of his cassock and handed it to Ratzinger with the request that he peruse it in peace and quiet. When he opened the letter, he was thunderstruck: it was his appointment as the new Archbishop of Munich and Freising. That did not suit him at all. He was up to his ears in work and, besides, did not feel equal to this challenge. Before he answered, he was allowed at least to consult a man whom he trusted, namely, Professor Johann Auer, who knew his colleague's strengths and weaknesses and was a realist. Therefore his answer surprised Ratzinger all the more: "Joseph, you must accept" (M 152). After some hesitation and with a heavy heart, he then consented.

I was just as surprised by the news. I happened to be on tour and only learned about it all by telephone. The only thing I remember is how his appointment as Archbishop of Munich and Freising was announced. It was on March 25, 1977, on the feast of the Annunciation, and we were having a concert in Munich, in the church of Saint Anthony. At twelve o'clock noon, the bells throughout the city tolled. It was very moving, I must say.

Before he went to Munich, he celebrated his farewell Mass in Regensburg, in the parish church in Ziegetsdorf. A junior choir of the Regensburg Domspatzen sang at it. It was a moving farewell. But at least this time he was not all that far away.

The new Archbishop of Munich, Joseph Ratzinger, receives the document certifying his appointment

Only a good hour-and-a-half drive separate Regensburg and Munich from each other.

On the eve of Pentecost, May 28, 1977, in the Liebfrauendom, the Cathedral of Our Lady in Munich, Joseph Ratzinger was consecrated Archbishop of Munich and Freising. Just as he said later as pope, he thought then, too, that the jubilation with which he was greeted had nothing to do with him personally: "I was being greeted as bishop, as bearer of the Mystery of Christ, even if the majority were not explicitly conscious of this. The joy of the day was something really different from approval of a particular person, whose qualifications still had to be demonstrated. It was joy over the fact that this office, this service, was again present in a person who does not act and live for himself but for Him and therefore for all" (M 153).

And then he said something that by all means could be cited three decades later as the program for his pontificate as well: "The bishop does not act in his own name but, rather, is the trustee of someone else, of Jesus Christ and his Church. He is not a manager, a boss in his own right, but rather the delegate of someone else, whose place he takes. Hence he cannot arbitrarily change his opinion and advocate one thing today and something else tomorrow, depending on how promising it seems. He is not there to spread his own private ideas but, rather, is an envoy who has to deliver a message that is greater than he. He is measured by this fidelity; that is his task" (H 208).

He inscribed "Co-workers of the Truth" on his coat of arms as his episcopal motto. The truth was what he had sought throughout his life and had finally found in Christ. The coat of arms itself was made up of three fields. The first shows the Moor of Freising, the ancient symbol of the cathedral city, for him *"a sign of the universality of the Church"* (M 154). The second field shows a shell, the sign of man's pilgrimage, but also connected with a story that is told about Saint Augustine. Once, while Augustine was pondering the mystery of the Trinity, he saw a child on the seashore playing with a shell, with which he was trying to scoop up the water of the sea and pour it into a little hole. Then he realized: your intellect can no more comprehend the mystery of God than that hole can contain the water of the sea. Thus the shell became for him a symbol of the greatness of the mystery that extends farther than all human knowledge. In the third field, he placed the bear of Saint Corbinian, which appeared on the coat of arms of the founding bishop of Freising. On a journey to Rome, so the legend goes, a bear mauled the saint's horse. Then Corbinian reprimanded it sternly and as a punishment strapped his pack onto its back, which the bear now had to carry to Rome.

Joseph Ratzinger was not a complacent bishop. He knew that Augustine despised shepherds who *"are like mute dogs; in order to avoid conflicts, they let the poison spread"* (SE 82). Peace is not the first duty of a bishop. The Church, he believed, cannot ally herself with the spirit of the age. So he castigated the *"pollution of the intellectual environment"* in our time, the *"fatty degeneration of the heart thanks to wealth and hedonism"* and the *"capitalistic lust for profit"*, but also the *"unleashing of violence, the reduction of human beings to the*

state of barbarians" (ST 68–69). Although conservative politicians bris-
tled, he called for Bavaria to take in Vietnamese refugees; not to do so
would be "a terrible shame" for a rich country. The most urgent task of
Christians, he preached, was "to recover the ability to be non-conformist,
that is, the ability to oppose a whole number of developments in our con-
temporary culture" (ST 69). A Christian cannot be someone who adapts
to everything, a moral coward. He must be courageous and inconvenient
and willing to bother people once in a while when necessary. The future
Benedict XVI never stood for a Catholicism that lets its little flag flutter
in the wind of the zeitgeist; *he stands for values.*

One important task for German Catholics in those days was recon-
ciliation with Poland. Eventually there were reciprocal visits of the Ger-
man and Polish bishops, during which Karol Wojtyla, who had meanwhile
been appointed a cardinal, met Ratzinger as a brother bishop. The
"uncomplicated human directness and openness and . . . the warmth" of
the man from Krakow impressed the German. "One sensed that this is
a man of God" (ST 72).

Only three months after his installation as a bishop, Pope Paul VI
appointed Archbishop Ratzinger, who had just turned fifty, a cardinal.
In that capacity, he helped elect the successor of Peter two times in
1978, only a few weeks apart—first, John Paul I and, then, after his
sudden heart attack and death after exactly thirty-three days, John
Paul II. Only two years after his election as the 264th successor of Peter,
the Pope from Poland decided to visit Germany. One of his destinations
was Munich, and his host there was Joseph Cardinal Ratzinger.

At that time I met for the first time the great Pole about whom
my brother had told me so much—and I was profoundly
impressed. He radiated so much: on the one hand, an impressive
dignity, but not like Cardinal Faulhaber, who always seemed somehow distant. With John Paul II, it was a dignity that at the same
time demanded closeness and was marked by kindness and friendliness. That resulted in a wonderful mixture that made him a
sympathetic figure from the start.

During that papal visit in Munich, we also had the privilege of singing: a meeting between the Pope and artists took place, at which the Bavarian Radio Choir also sang and, of course, the Regensburg Domspatzen. That was a great experience for the boys. Today I still have a whole series of photos of it. This first visit of a pope to Germany in hundreds of years was for us and for everybody concerned about the Church a brand-new situation. Previously the pope was an institution that seemed far, far away, up high, miles removed from our daily routine. Then suddenly to have him in our midst, to meet him in our everyday world, our homeland, was an extraordinary experience: suddenly in Munich we were face to face with the pope!

Evidently Pope Wojtyla got along so well with his host in Munich that he summoned him one year later to Rome. He was to become the new Prefect of the Congregation for the Doctrine of the Faith, the same Vatican dicastery that his criticism at the Second Vatican Council had so decisively helped to reform. Again Ratzinger hesitated, looking for all sorts of excuses. First he said that he could not simply leave his diocese in the lurch. Then he considered it unwise that he, a theologian of all people, should judge the works of other theologians—he could quickly be accused of partisanship. How could this official, high-ranking position alongside the pope be combined with his work as a writer? How would it look if he now headed the very same Vatican office that had just forbidden his ex-colleague Hans Küng to teach as a Catholic theologian? And as a Bavarian with close ties to his homeland, would he be able to manage in Rome at all? John Paul II would not let loose. And finally, when the Pope had just survived the attempt on his life, Cardinal Ratzinger gave in. Together with his sister, Maria, who now as before kept house for him, he moved in 1982 to the Tiber, while Georg Ratzinger remained in Regensburg.

Well, I knew that my advice in this case did not matter. I regretted it very much, I must honestly say, that my brother now had to move far away again. At the time, I even asked Cardinal Höffner whether he might not be able to apply the brakes. But he only admired him because he was going to Rome now. For me that was something negative at first. I was just sad, because the great closeness that had existed previously between us was no longer possible now. Of course, as always we spent our vacation together. On All Saints' Day, at first he merely sent our sister to visit our parents' grave. Only after she died (*1991*) did he come again himself. At Christmas, or more precisely after the holidays, he always spent a few days in Regensburg, then again around the Ascension, and finally during the summer. I in turn spent my vacation as often as possible with him in Rome. Our closeness as siblings therefore was not suspended; opportunities always arose to spend time together. So then I gradually became accustomed to the new situation and in some areas even found positive elements in it.

But I think he was not eager at all to go to Rome right away. He actually wanted to convince the Pope to leave him in Munich, and again and again he gave him good reasons to do so. But John Paul II only said that Munich was important but Rome was even more important, and that settled the matter for him.

In fact, my brother had a new, major, and very important task there. His predecessor, Cardinal Ottaviani (*1890–1979*), had not had a very positive reputation. At that time, people had the impression that the Holy Office, as it was still called in his day, actually steered opinion a bit too narrow-mindedly. Later, I understood that this was a mistake that arose only from a particular perspective but was not accurate. Whenever there is order somewhere, then there are always those who disturb that order, do not understand it, or else deliberately refuse to accept it. I only gradually became aware of the fact that order, in the sense of clarity and truth, must then be created over and over again. The motto that my brother had selected already as Archbishop of Munich, "Cooperatores veritatis", was to that extent programmatic and directly addressed this point and his task in Rome.

John Paul II, who had read every single Ratzinger book in the original language and was much better acquainted with the German than the latter was with him, demonstrated excellent leadership qualities with his choice. Ratzinger complemented him perfectly and embodied everything that he was not. For no two men could have been more different than the athletic Pole and the delicate German. The charismatic, extroverted "John Paul Superstar" was a "pope you can touch" who wanted to embrace the whole world—whereas Ratzinger was always a quiet, introverted individual, a timid man with a fine intellect who shied away from publicity. The one was a mystic and a poet, the other a theologian and an analytic mind. The great heart of the Church and her razor-sharp intellect: the weaknesses of the one were the strengths of the other.

With German thoroughness, Ratzinger devoted himself to his new task. First, he rejuvenated and internationalized his congregation, appointed canon lawyers and theologians from all five continents who had just come from the university. Ultimately, his staff consisted of thirty-nine regular co-workers. The working relationship was collegial. For each one he had an open ear, and important questions were often discussed in a small circle during the coffee break, where the exchange could become quite controversial. One close collaborator said: "It never mattered to him if someone called his opinion into question. He was anything but stubborn and always willing to admit a mistake. He listened to his interlocutor patiently and thoroughly, then carefully formulated his response in prose that was always ready to print. When he wrote, he wrote the clean copy immediately, without having to revise it even once, such was his concentration on what he was doing. In a certain way he is a genius."

The Romans loved him even in those days because he never took himself too seriously. They knew that he rose in the morning around six and went to sleep in the evening at around ten. They saw how he walked to work every morning across Saint Peter's Square with his worn-out leather briefcase under his arm. When tourists took him for a routine priest and asked him something, he answered in a friendly way. Since he speaks ten languages, he could say something to anyone, and his French is so good that many a tourist thought he was a Frenchman.

"Father, do you know where the pope lives?" "Yes, up there. The last three windows of the top story." "Thank you, Father. We wish we could be there now. Don't you?" The Cardinal laughed slyly but said nothing. He used to see the Pope at least once a week.

In the afternoon, he would stroll through the old quarter across from Saint Peter's Square, the "Borgo Pio", where he knew everybody. Often he would stop to greet the shop owners. A Bavarian in Rome. His favorite restaurant was still the Cantina Tirolese, where there was hearty Alpine food at low prices, for instance, dumplings or goulash with sausages. Yet he abstained almost entirely from alcohol. The Italians watched with mild horror as he ordered a glass of orange juice even with fish. His pride and joy were the flowerbeds on the terrace of his simply furnished apartment. His passion was his piano, on which he played Mozart to relax. His heart, however, belonged to the cats of the district. Thus "il tedesco", "the German", slowly became a Roman among Romans. The neighbors generously overlooked the thing about the wine.

He did not change much in Rome; over the years, he was actually very constant and always remained true to himself. I do not know how he adjusted to the work; I deliberately did not meddle in his professional duties. But other than that, it was not such a big change at all. He systematically continued along his path, even though it was now for a different goal and in a different style. He succeeded at that rather harmoniously.

He had a very good relationship with the Pope; every Friday he went to his apartments for an audience. In the Vatican it is arranged so that on Mondays the Cardinal Secretary of State visits the Pope, on Tuesdays the second-in-command from the Secretariat of State, and so forth. On each day of the week, a different high-ranking Curia official comes for an audience and to give a report, and on Fridays the Prefect of the Congregation for the Doctrine of the Faith had his turn. I often accompanied him on his walk as far as the entrance to the Vatican at the Porta Sant' Anna. But he never spoke much about it. He esteemed

John Paul II very highly, not only his kindness and humanity, indeed, his almost fatherly character, but also his erudition.

It is only partially true that he used to feed the cats in his neighborhood. Roman cats are all very shy. On the other hand, it is true, and there are witnesses, to the following: every Thursday he used to celebrate early morning Mass in the Campo Santo, the church of the German cemetery on the grounds of the Vatican, and a cat would sit there in the cemetery and wait for him. It was there only on Thursdays. German theologians are lodged in the adjacent building, and they observed this: every Thursday at around the time when he would arrive there, the cat was waiting at the entrance to the Campo Santo to be petted! I must admit that we Ratzingers all like cats very much. A well-behaved "pussycat" is nice to have around! But, as I said, Roman cats are usually very shy.

Now there is another story about my brother having a special relationship with Chico, the tomcat belonging to our neighbor, Herr Hofbauer, but that is not true at all. Chico actually can be rather nasty. At the start he was quite nice, but by now he is rather old and can get quite vicious, and then he scratches and bites. Once my brother was in his house in Pentling, and Chico crept in. Then when my brother wanted to leave, he did not dare carry the tomcat out himself; he called Herr Hofbauer, who had to come and fetch his Chico. For he himself would at most pet him, but no more than that.... That Chico is simply a difficult animal with two souls in his breast.

Cardinal Ratzinger's job in Rome was to define, disseminate, and defend the doctrine of the Catholic Church. He was not entitled to take any unauthorized actions. What the Church believes is laid down both in Sacred Scripture and in an almost two-thousand-year-old doctrinal tradition. In order to make a reliable summary of this teaching readily available to believers throughout the world, John Paul II commissioned him in 1986 to compose an authoritative catechism. After five years of work [by an international team of authors and editors] the volume was ready to be issued in 1991. "Of course, it's a book produced by human beings that can always be improved," Ratzinger said, "but it is a good book" (SE 92). It became a worldwide best-seller; in the United States alone more than two million copies were sold. Further documents, for instance, a commentary on the "Third Secret of Fatima" that was first made public in the year 2000 or the declaration Dominus Iesus, *were published at the Pope's behest.*

Ratzinger's team was responsible for making sure that the teaching of the Catholic Church was neither diluted nor distorted. If an official representative of the Catholic Church wrote something that was not in keeping with her clearly defined doctrine, then this had to be pointed out to him. If a professor being paid by the Church who was supposed to be training the next generation of priests was teaching his own version of Christianity, then that contradicted his employment contract. In any business in the world, it is taken for granted that every co-worker has to abide by the policies of the firm, and those who do not are fired, but when the Church tried to deal with such problems in a similar way, this led to indignation and attacks. The scapegoat then was always Ratzinger, whom the press alternately called "God's watchdog", "Panzerkardinal", and "Great Inquisitor". "There are nice watchdogs, too", he once commented with warm humor.

As Prefect, he was never one of those people who are intent on putting others down. "He always spoke in a soft, gentle tone of voice. He never got loud, never gave the impression of being annoyed or furious", one of his closest co-workers told me. "He is a man without prejudices and ready in principle to speak with anyone. He respects every human being and never attacked the person per se but only an idea he considered wrong. He avoided quarrels and, instead, used to invite an opponent to a meal, so as then to explain to him quite calmly and in great detail where he was wrong, in his opinion. This all happened in a peaceful, friendly, modest way, without anyone having to feel injured or attacked."

Nevertheless, a certain distorted image developed even in ecclesiastical circles, especially in Germany. Anyone who did not dare to attack the beloved, charismatic John Paul II made Ratzinger his "shadow". "The Pope would like to," the story then went, "but Ratzinger does not let him." This was sheer nonsense, as insiders always knew. "John Paul II was much too much of a stubborn Pole to allow anyone to tell him what to do," a co-worker said, "much less would Ratzinger have ventured to dictate something to the Pope. He respected him much too much for that, and he considered himself much too unimportant."

Ratzinger was never a man for politics or intrigue. He always refrained from building up a dynastic power for himself, never pulled strings, and as a matter of principle rejected secretive ties with special groups that considered themselves the new elite. Power, career, and influence had never interested him. His world was books, his goal: the exploration of truth; his life revolved around the faith. Anyone who ever saw him vested for Mass and lined up with other cardinals could see the innocence in his almost childlike features, the simple devotion of his piously folded hands. "He is a man of prayer, one of the few who deserve the adjective 'God-fearing' and celebrate Mass with real fervor —a true priest", the aforementioned co-worker confided to me.

Of course he suffered from the attacks; it is not as if they did not matter to him; he does react to such things. But I never spoke to him about them. Through our very natural, relaxed time together, as it always was, I wanted to push such things into the background and to enable him to gain a certain interior distance from them. At least with me, he should enjoy the normal life he knew and loved. This was especially true after our sister died.

During his first years in Rome, he always used to send her, as I mentioned, to Regensburg for the Feast of All Saints to visit the grave of our parents. In 1991, too, she went back to Pentling and, of course, lived in my brother's house. On the day after her arrival, the neighbors phoned me and told me that my sister was sick. Naturally I drove there immediately and alerted the doctor, who determined that it was a heart attack. We called for an ambulance, which brought her to the hospital of the Brothers of

Mercy. At first they said it was a serious heart attack but that she would get over it soon. But then, on November 2, 1991, I was not allowed to go to her room. They told me I should first report to the doctor. She told me my sister had suffered a massive brain hemorrhage and was unconscious. On that same day, in the late afternoon, she died from that hemorrhage. Of course my brother came to Regensburg right away. The Pontifical Requiem took place on November 8, 1991, in the Regensburg Cathedral, and afterward she was buried in our parents' grave in the cemetery in Ziegetsdorf.

In her obituary, it said that "for thirty-four years she served her brother Joseph at all the stages of his career with tireless devotion and great kindness and humility."

My brother himself was sick at that time. He suffered from constant headaches and happened to be spending a few days with nuns in the vicinity of the airport. Maria had therefore booked only a one-way flight to Regensburg and intended to plan the return flight separately, because she feared that something could happen to him and he might need her care. In reality, she then died, not he. I do not know whether this fatal blow welded us brothers even closer together, whether it further deepened our good relationship or not. In any case, we knew that from now on we had only the two of us; our family had again become smaller by one member.

After that we intensified even more our efforts to spend our vacation together. There were certain localities we always liked to visit. One of them was Brixen in South Tyrol; we always enjoyed traveling there. Another was Hofgastein (Austria)—he had met the pastor of that locality at a lecture. We also liked to visit the Petrinum, a minor seminary and *gymnasium* in Linz (Austria). Naturally he always had a pile of work with him, correspondence, and God knows what else.

Nevertheless, we usually had enough time for extended walks and excursions. We were often invited, for instance from Brixen or Linz, to visit some place or other. They would send us a car, and then we always liked to see the sights there. Other than that, we just celebrated Mass together and then had breakfast. In the mornings he would work, and then we had our midday meal, and in the afternoon we went for a walk, if he did not have to work again. Usually, though, it was a lighter daily schedule and a nice time.

In addition, he came to Regensburg regularly, of course, usually three or four times a year. Then we often ate at his place, in his house in Pentling. Fortunately, dear nuns always put something in the refrigerator, because neither of us is a very great cook. Afterward, he washed the dishes and I dried. Then we usually took a little walk and talked meanwhile about God and the world, the news of the day and everyday things. He was very attached to the house, and so, even when he was back in Rome, I would often drive to Pentling on Sundays to check for him whether everything was in order. Usually I telephoned him from there and told him right away that "the house is still standing" and that he had nothing to worry about.

In 1994, after thirty years with the Domspatzen, I bid them farewell. My brother came especially for this occasion to Regensburg, celebrated Solemn High Mass in the cathedral, and gave a beautiful sermon. It was a festive event; every seat in the cathedral was occupied. At the conclusion, the choir, under the direction of a singer from the Mendelssohn Chorus, sang "Denn er hat seinen Engeln befohlen", a piece that actually is always performed only for very special occasions. There was thunderous applause afterward. That was followed by another celebration, a reception in the Kolping House, at which my brother gave the formal address. There was already a rather melancholy farewell mood, but I was prepared for it. I had already turned seventy, and it is usual for a seventy-year-old

priest to go into retirement. So then I followed suit. When the
boys went on vacation soon afterward, I took care of moving,
together with Frau Heindl, whom I had already hired at the
time and who has been my housekeeper ever since.

At that time, I did not want to move to Rome, and even
today I have no intention of doing so. Rents there are very high;
it is difficult to get a halfway decent apartment; and besides, I
speak only a few bits and pieces of Italian. I had actually hoped
that my brother would regularly come visit, and that would have
been enough for me.

For that was actually his plan. He never wanted to come back
to Germany, not even after his retirement, which he hoped to
take in 2002. He simply did not want to transport over the Alps
the pile of books he had collected in the meantime. Then too,
in Pentling he would never have had enough room for that many
books. Instead, he wanted to keep living in Rome but also to
come more often to Germany and for a longer time, so that we
could be together more. Moreover, he intended to write a few
more books and to finish other works he had not yet completed. But John Paul II simply did not let him go. Again and
again, he asked him to stay in office. And then came the conclave that definitively ruled out all his plans for the future.

Thus the bear of Saint Corbinian, which he already had on
his coat of arms as Archbishop of Munich and Freising, in fact
became a symbol of his career. It is funny how bears have always
played a special role in his life. Starting in 1928, when as a little
boy in Marktl he fell in love with the teddy bear in the store
window, which he then received as a Christmas present, and
later another bear that was a little bit bigger. He liked them very
much, his teddy bears; they were always dear and precious to
him, so that the bear had a certain place in our family, a very
congenial place. And then it turned out well that in the story of
Corbinian, a bear appeared again, which at first was the villain
and mauled the saint's pack animal. But then Saint Corbinian

evidently reprimanded it so vehemently that the bear felt regret and carried the Bishop's baggage to Rome. That is a nice story and at the same time a metaphor for my brother's life, who as Archbishop of Munich and Freising was not only the successor of Saint Corbinian but also the first of his successors who was summoned to Rome permanently, who remained there and was elected the successor of Saint Peter. The bear got his freedom back, but he must carry the burden the dear Lord has imposed on him to the very end. Yet this burden is rich in blessings!

When Pope Benedict XVI visited his Bavarian homeland in September 2006, he took up the image of Corbinian's bear and explained it with the words of Saint Augustine, "I have become for you a beast of burden, but as such 'I am always with you' (Ps 73:23)", as a metaphor for his own ministry. For precisely by carrying the burden, the Pope said, the animal remains constantly near his employer. Thus the bear encourages him "to carry out my ministry with confidence and joy . . . and to say my daily 'yes' to God. . . . Saint Corbinian's bear was set free in Rome. In my case, the Lord decided otherwise."

IX

Pope
(2005 to the present)

Like probably most Catholics, I, too, attentively followed the last days of John Paul II. I was aware that a great life was coming to an end in a completely organic way. Everyone sensed that he would not recover again from this final illness, yet it was all the more admirable how patiently and calmly he endured it. He even cheered up the people who had come to Rome, and somehow, for all his despondency about his own helplessness, he also radiated joy and confidence that he would soon be with his Heavenly Father. So it was a worthy end of a great personage, whose work was to continue from now on "over there".

What I admired very much were the many young people who spontaneously set out for Rome so as to manifest once more their solidarity with this great pope. It is always said that the youth want nothing to do with the Church, but this was strikingly disproved at that time. On the contrary, there are many young people, too, who are spontaneously attracted by the Church, once they have experienced that the everyday routine cannot answer their questions and cannot give any meaning to their lives, that this other thing, faith, is needed for that.

During the next two weeks, I was repeatedly asked by people, and by journalists too, whether my brother would become pope. My answer was always the same: "No, he certainly will not!" The conclave would never elect a man at his age—he was just turning seventy-eight. It was different in the case of John XXIII, because his predecessor, Pius XII, had not held a consistory during his last five years in office and had not appointed any new cardinals. The College of Cardinals was therefore more or less aging then, so that they were forced to elect an older candidate, who at the age of seventy-six, almost seventy-seven, was nevertheless a good year younger than my brother at the time of the 2005 conclave. Now, though, the College of Cardinals was as strong as it had ever been at a conclave; there had never been so many cardinals. There were many great and talented men of all ages among them, so there was really no need to elect one of the oldest. Therefore, it was quite clear to me that a younger man would be the next pope.

I even experienced the "Habemus Papam" live. At the time I was called by a journalist who said she had just heard that white smoke had gone up in Rome and wanted to hear from me whether I knew anything more specific. "No," I answered truthfully, "I know nothing." Then I turned on the television and heard it there, like everybody else.

That was on April 19, 2005, the second day of the conclave. After the new pope had accepted his election, the paper ballots were burned at 5:40 P.M., and white smoke was supposed to rise out of the chimney of the Sistine Chapel.

But the smoke was gray at first; there had been difficulties in lighting the fire. The faithful who had gathered on Saint Peter's Square and the four thousand or so representatives of the world press who were in Rome were still puzzling over the color of the smoke signal when at 6:06 P.M. the bells of Saint Peter's rang. Now everyone knew—and tens of thousands streamed onto Saint Peter's Square.

At 6:40 P.M. the Chilean Cardinal Jorge Medina Estévez stepped through the heavy red velvet curtains of the loggia of Saint Peter's Basilica. First he greeted the crowd in French, Italian, and German, only to continue then with the ancient Latin formula: "Annuntio vobis gaudium magnum: habemus Papam!" (I bring you good news of a great joy: we have a Pope!) There was great jubilation before the Chilean went on and gave the first name of the one who had been elected: "Eminentissimum ac

*Reverendissimum Dominum, Dominum Josephum." Here he paused so
as to heighten the suspense ...*

When the name "Josephum", Joseph, was mentioned, I froze
deep inside. I knew it was getting dangerous now, and I was in
suspense as to how things would continue.

*Then the rest of the announcement followed: "Sanctae Romanae Eccle-
siae Cardinalem Ratzinger".*

Then in fact the name Ratzinger was mentioned! I must quite
honestly say that at that moment I was rather disheartened. It
was a great challenge, an enormous task for him, I thought, and
I was seriously worried. I saw neither the pomp nor the beauty
of it, but only the challenge of this office, which now demanded
everything of him, and the burden it meant for him. And I was
sad that now he would probably have no more time for me. So
that evening I went to bed rather depressed. Throughout that
evening and then again well into the following afternoon the
telephone rang nonstop, yet now it did not matter to me at all.
I simply did not answer. "Nuts to you", I thought to myself!
I did not call him, either. I told myself I would not reach him
now anyway, so many people were around him at the moment
who all wanted something from him. He called then the next
morning, or rather: he tried to call me, but because the telephone in my house was ringing constantly and getting on my
nerves, I did not answer it. "Keep on ringing, you can ring
without me, too", I thought, while it may have been my brother
calling! At some point, Frau Heindl, my housekeeper, answered
the telephone, and so he had her on the line first and not me.
She was naturally somewhat shocked that this stubborn caller
was none other than the Pope. If I remember correctly, she was
not even able to connect me with him, for some reason. At any
rate, it was some time before we were finally able to speak with

each other. Now, thank God, I have a second telephone upstairs in the living room. An acquaintance arranged this for me when he learned that I got calls from so many people that I sometimes did not answer when it was my brother on the line. He alone knows the number for this second line. When this telephone rings, then I know that my brother, the Pope, is calling me. But at that time, of course, I did not yet have it.

On the telephone, he already seemed quite calm again. At the moment of his election, however, he told me, it had struck him like a bolt of lightning. It was so unforeseeable, it came so suddenly in the voting, that the working of the Holy Spirit was obvious. He then surrendered quickly to him, because he, too, recognized God's will in it.

Now that Joseph Cardinal Ratzinger had been elected the 265th successor of Saint Peter, Jesus' prophecy, which was actually about the martyrdom of the Prince of the Apostles in Rome, sounded as though it was also intended for him: "When you are old, you will stretch out your hands, and another will fasten your belt for you and carry you where you do not wish to go" (Jn 21:18).

For again, as always in his life, it was someone else who led him where he really did not want to go. When Benedict XVI celebrated his first Mass as pope on the morning of April 20, 2005, he remembered his beloved predecessor once again. After the cardinals had elected him, he said, "I seemed to see his smiling eyes and hear his words, at this moment addressed specifically to me, 'Do not be afraid.'" A strong hand was clasping his and was now driving him on to complete what John Paul II began: a Church that, according to Christ's teaching and example, "looks serenely at the past and is not afraid of the future".

Five days later, in his address to the German pilgrims who had come to his installation, he became even clearer—and chose a telling metaphor: "When, little by little, the trend of the voting led me to understand that, to say it simply, the axe was going to fall on me, my head began to spin. I was convinced that I had already carried out my life's work and could look forward to ending my days peacefully. With profound conviction I said to the Lord: Do not do this to me! You have younger and better people at your disposal, who can face this great responsibility with greater dynamism and greater strength.

"I was then very touched by a brief note written to me by a brother Cardinal. He reminded me that on the occasion of the Mass for John Paul II, I had based my homily, starting from the Gospel, on the Lord's words to Peter by the Lake of Gennesaret: 'Follow me!' I spoke of how again and again, Karol Wojtyla received this call from the Lord, and how each time he had to renounce much and to simply say: Yes, I will follow you, even if you lead me where I never wanted to go. This brother Cardinal wrote to me: Were the Lord to say to you now, 'Follow me', then remember what you preached. Do not refuse! Be obedient in the same way that you described the great Pope, who has returned to the house of the Father. This deeply moved me. The ways of the Lord are not easy, but we were not created for an easy life, but for great things, for goodness."

Shortly afterward, Bishop Müller (*Bishop Gerhard Ludwig Müller of the Regensburg Diocese*) called and invited me to travel with him to my brother's installation, and of course I gladly accepted. So I had the privilege of driving with His Excellency to the airport and flew with him to Rome as part of the delegation from Regensburg.

In Rome, then, I lived first in the old cardinal's apartment belonging to my brother, since he was still staying together with the other cardinals in the Vatican guest house, the "Domus Sanctae Marthae" (Saint Martha's House)—for security reasons; he had to be guarded, after all. The apartment was directly opposite the Apostolic Palace, but outside the Vatican City State, on the Piazza Città Leonina. The next morning I picked him up, and then we drove together to his apartment. A gigantic crowd of people had gathered in front of it, and they applauded immediately; he greeted them briefly, and then we went in.

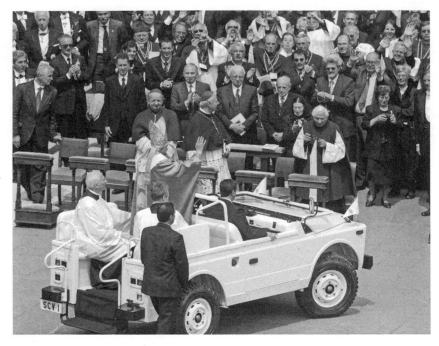

Georg Ratzinger at his brother's installation on April 24, 2005

Has he changed? Was he still the same old Joseph, or could one sense the working of the Holy Spirit, this new charism that many people claim to have noticed in him?

Of course, he was still the same old Joseph, and he still is today. The working of the Holy Spirit is limited to his official activity, but as a human being he has not changed. He does not stand on ceremony, does not try to be pretentious. He presents himself as who he is and does not want to slip into a role or wear a mask, as others may do. When Peter Seewald, for instance, describes him as a "charismatic pope" with a great influence on the world, then I must say he quite certainly does not exercise that influence consciously. Perhaps it is, after all, the influence of the Holy Spirit that lends him a certain charisma at his public appearances. Otherwise, he is now as before the kindly, friendly, and modest man he always was, quite unaffected and cordial.

Has he confided in you why he chose the papal name Benedict? Was it his reverence for Saint Benedict of Nursia (480–547), founder of the great religious order and father of Western monasticism, or was his namesake the intellectual Pope Benedict XIV (1740–1758), or the pope of peace, Benedict XV (1914–1922)?

I myself do not know. But we did once talk about papal names, and he simply said that Benedict was a nice name. That was in a very general conversation that was not at all related to him personally; he felt this name was nice and suitable for a pope, in terms of its sound as well as its meaning: "the Blessed one" (from Latin *benedicere* = to bless) who is also a blessing for others. Naturally, he holds Saint Benedict in very, very high esteem. Of course he knows that the other two were great popes, but he never actually spoke about them. Therefore I would rather say that Saint Benedict of Nursia was the namesake but that there were also aesthetic and etymological reasons that led to his choice of this name.

Since then a special apartment has been set up for the Pope's brother in the guest wing of the Apostolic Palace. In the summer, however, he lives with his brother in the papal summer residence in Castel Gandolfo.

During my next visit in the summer of 2005, I think I gave him a good scare. It was on August 3 around noon, and I was just listening to a CD with a fugue from the *Hammerklavier* Sonata by Beethoven, when suddenly everything around me started spinning. For a short space of time I was out of it but, soon afterward, fully conscious again. When this happened again during the evening meal, my brother and the whole dinner party were very upset. He asked his personal physician, Doctor

Renato Buzzonetti, to examine me, and the latter had me admitted right away to the Gemelli Clinic in Rome, where they implanted a pacemaker in me. As I was staying there, they told me: "The Pope is coming to visit you!" Among the employees of the hospital, the nurses and the doctors, it was as though a bomb had hit. Some said that now they themselves needed coronary treatment! He took the helicopter to travel from Castel Gandolfo to Rome simply because the Roman officials prefer it. If he were to travel by automobile, it would disrupt the local traffic on account of the security measures. I was very happy about his visit, but of course a pope never comes alone. The Prefect, Archbishop Harvey, and his secretary, Doctor Gänswein, were there, too, a whole platoon that turned the hospital visit into a major event. At any rate, we were able to spend a good quarter hour alone before the television cameras arrived, too.

Then in October 2005, the Regensburg Domspatzen visited Rome. They were so happy to have the privilege of giving a concert in the Sistine Chapel (*on October 22*), for there is probably no more magnificent or inspiring setting; moreover, it has magnificent acoustics. The enormous excitement was palpable, and everyone gave his very best. The Holy Father was certainly very happy about this visit from his homeland.

One year later, in September 2006, Benedict XVI returned, perhaps for the last time, to his Bavarian homeland. Whereas usually he never goes along on a papal journey, this time Georg Ratzinger could not pass up the opportunity to accompany him to one of the most important places of their childhood.

When my brother came to Altötting, naturally I traveled there from Regensburg. I stayed overnight with the Capuchins and ate with them. Before the papal Mass, I met Professor Franz Mussner (*b. 1916*), who taught New Testament exegesis in Regensburg and today lives in Passau, his native city, as a cathedral canon. At that time,

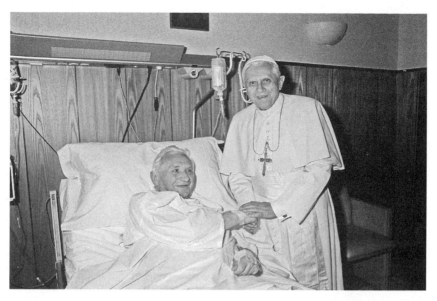

August 5, 2005: The Pope visits his brother, Georg, in the Gemelli Clinic

he had just celebrated his ninetieth birthday, and when he saw me, he said we two were the only ones who had permission to carry a cane; all the other attendees were forbidden to have one for security reasons. A very festive, beautiful liturgy followed, which visibly moved people. Then during the meal afterward, crispy roast pork and dumplings, I finally sat at a table again with my brother. Instead of taking a siesta afterward, we took a little walk through the convent garden and "chatted". My brother was so happy he could finally be in his homeland again.

At that time he presented to Our Lady of Altötting his bishop's ring, which Maria and I had given him when he was consecrated a bishop. I had kept it for all those years, until Sister Birgit, a Schönstatt nun who serves as a secretary to my brother, suggested to him that he give this ring to Our Lady of Altötting. Then she asked me what I thought of the idea. "I certainly approve," I replied, "for if someday I pass on, then it would be lying around somewhere, but there it is in a safe place: the Mother

of God can look after it best." I was very happy about this suggestion and wholeheartedly approved of it. So I brought the ring
to my brother in Altötting, and he laid it down there in the
Chapel of Graces.

Next on the itinerary after Altötting was Marktl, where we
visited Saint Oswald's, the church where he was baptized. In
quiet prayer, we lingered there in front of the baptismal font
over which he had been accepted into the communion of Holy
Mother Church seventy-nine years before. After that, he took
me with him in the helicopter to Regensburg; I sat opposite
him, face-to-face, the whole time.

The welcome in Regensburg was overwhelming. I spent the
night in the major seminary beside my brother's apartment, for
the next morning we wanted to celebrate early Mass together.
From there we set out for the great papal Mass on Islinger Feld.
On the program that afternoon were his address in the aula magna
of the university and an ecumenical evening prayer service. And
then finally came September 13, to which we had looked forward for so long. Already when the program for his trip to Germany was being planned, my brother asked for a day he could
use for private meetings. On that day, he was with me practically the whole time. There was only one official item on the
program at 11:00 in the morning: the consecration of the new
organ in the "Old Chapel", of which I had grown so fond that
this, too, was actually a private event. Originally he was supposed to travel directly from the major seminary, where he was
staying overnight, to the "Old Chapel" on Schwarze-Bären-
Straße, but he wanted to drop off something at my house first.
So we went there via Luzengasse, which runs by my house. At
the time, we thought we would use the nearest entrance to the
church, but the chapter of the "Old Chapel" was waiting for us
on the north side, and so we entered by the north side, were
solemnly greeted there, and arrived punctually for the great consecration of the organ. After that, we returned to my house.

Along the way, we met the leader of the Jewish community, Herr Hans Rosengold (who has unfortunately died since), whom my brother thanked for his hospitality—he had invited the whole papal entourage to dinner.

Upstairs on the terrace of my house, we drank an aperitif and then ate our midday meal on the ground floor. The Bishop was there and also a small group including his secretary, Monsignor Gänswein. Frau Heindl, my housekeeper, had prepared a delicious meal for us, which in fact almost did not arrive at our table. You see, she lives right across the street on Königsstraße and had cooked there for us in advance because she thought that that was the simplest solution: then she would just have to bring the food over quickly, as she often did. But on that day, our street was blocked off, and the police did not want to let her through. Then dear Frau Heindl became rather indignant: "There's no bomb in the pot, but soup for the Holy Father! And if you don't let me through, then he gets nothing to eat!" she said very energetically. Then the policemen themselves were disconcerted and did not know at first whether they should believe her. So they did not leave her side but came into the house with her as far as the kitchen, where they then saw that what she said was true, that she was practically at home here and was supposed to prepare the midday meal. Eventually there was *breznsuppe* (pretzel soup), roast beef smothered in onions, spätzle, and finally a pineapple custard; everything tasted wonderful.

After a little siesta, a midday nap, we drove up to Pentling to visit first of all the grave of our parents at the cemetery in Ziegetsdorf. The Bishop and his secretary came along, too. In Pentling, a whole crowd of people had gathered, among them Herr and Frau Hofbauer, who take perfect care of our house there—they are very fine people. Finally, in our house we ate supper. My brother also lay down for a short time before we drove back to the major seminary, because he was really very tired and had a headache. He enjoyed that day very much, and it was almost

Benedict XVI thanks Frau Agnes Heindl, his brother's housekeeper, for the good meal

like it always was. He loves the little house in Pentling very much; he really feels at home there, for even the most beautiful palace does not have what a one-family house like that has. Of course this visit to his homeland was primarily a pastoral journey, but for him it was also a farewell to his old life.

Since then he calls me several times a week; I never call him. After all, it is much simpler to reach me by telephone: I am almost always at home and have no daily routine to follow. He, on the other hand, almost always has deadlines or something to do, and so I would never dare to disturb him. So he calls me whenever he has time, and I wait for his call.

I visit him several times a year. Naturally I travel to Rome for Christmas, but not until December 28, when the church celebrations of Christmas are over, and then I stay until January 10. So we spend the feast of the Epiphany together, which in Italy is celebrated even more than in Germany; there, unlike at home, it is the time for exchanging gifts. I visit him the second time in the spring, sometime between April and June. In 2009, for instance, I was in Rome on Pentecost, when the Cologne Chamber Orchestra had the privilege of performing Haydn's *Harmony* Mass at the special liturgy on Pentecost Sunday in Saint Peter's Basilica. At the time, the conductor invited me, and of course I did not want to miss it. Then I always spend August or at least the better part of the month with my brother at his summer residence in Castel Gandolfo. And, finally, I am often in Rome again in October or November, when some major musical performance takes place to which I am invited. That was the case, for example, in October 2007, when the Symphony Orchestra and Choir of Bavarian Radio with chief conductor Mariss Jansons performed Beethoven's Ninth Symphony in the Paul VI Audience Hall.

I had spoken beforehand by telephone a few times with Herr Jansons, because my brother had requested that the motet "Tu es Petrus" by (*the Renaissance composer Giovanni Pierluigi da*) Palestrina (*ca. 1525–1594*) be sung, too. At first he did not want to do it, although he is a great conductor. Why, I do not know. He wanted to perform instead the "Ave verum" by Mozart, but any children's choir can sing that: we did not need the Radio Symphony Orchestra and Choir for that. In any case, he finally gave in, and it was a wonderful performance. Several former Domspatzen belong to the Radio Choir as well as to the orchestra, and in that way I met them again, which gave me great joy.

When I visit my brother, we talk about all sorts of topics: about the past, about the problems in today's world, about personal things, about health, and naturally about the weather occasionally, too.

How do you address him then?

I call him Joseph, of course; anything else would be abnormal!

Does he suffer intensely from the many attacks from the media also?

He is personally very sensitive, but he also knows from which corner these attacks come and the reason for them, what is usually behind them. That way he overcomes it more easily, he rises above it more simply. It is nevertheless true, too, that he most often meets with a lot of sympathy, again and again and wherever he goes.

Can you reveal to us his greatest wish?

Well, I really cannot mention one single specific wish. He simply hopes that he succeeds in completing his task as well as possible, that from the human side he can contribute his part to what the Holy Spirit is working from above.

In your view, what are the focal points of his pontificate?

The focal points result from particular situations to which he reacts, and therefore they are more reactive than active. But he is of course very concerned that the liturgy should be celebrated worthily and that it be celebrated correctly. Indeed, that is a genuine problem. Our diocesan music director recently said that it is by no means easy nowadays to find a church where the pastor celebrates his Mass according to the regulations of the Church. There are so many priests who think they have to add something here and change something there. So my brother wants an orderly, good liturgy that moves people interiorly and is understood as a call from God.

Do you see continuity between the pontificates of John Paul II and Benedict XVI, or is your brother focusing on different matters?

You cannot say that, because to a great extent pontificates are not defined by the will of the pope but, rather, are reactions and responses to the events of their time. Of course, the events of our time manifest a certain degree of continuity; there are no major leaps or breaks but, rather, problems that develop continuously over the decades.

No doubt, John Paul II took his inspiration from my brother in many areas and, of course, was in ongoing contact with him; he set great store by his judgment. In that regard, then, there is a certain similarity, and the two pontificates do not differ in essential points.

What does the Pope's normal daily routine look like?

Now, I do not know what all is supposed to be confidential, but I think I can speak about this. Early in the morning around 7:00, he celebrates Holy Mass in his private chapel, and afterward he makes a short meditation and, finally, prays the Breviary until breakfast at around 8:00. Until then, we are together, when I happen to be visiting him; then we say goodbye at that point in time, and each goes to his apartment.

Then he prepares for the events of the day, for instance, for the visitors he will receive in a personal audience: Who are they and what is their concern or the request they come to make? That, of course, requires a thorough preparation and an equally careful follow-up.

On Tuesdays, there is also the preparation for the large audience on Wednesday morning. For example, he has to practice the pronunciation of the foreign languages in which he will greet the pilgrims and the pilgrimage groups—of course, he does not speak them all fluently. For this purpose, he listens to the correct pronunciation on a tape and then practices it, so as to avoid making big mistakes and to be understood correctly.

At 1:15 P.M. on weekdays, the midday meal is served—on Sunday, earlier at 1:00—and afterward, he takes a short walk through the garden on the roof of the Apostolic Palace, because "Post coenam stabis vel passus mille meabis" (*After eating you should rest, or else walk a thousand steps*). Then comes the siesta, but he does not use the whole siesta time to rest; instead, he also writes letters and postcards and reads all sorts of things. I get the impression, in any case, that he works for part of the siesta time. In the summer, we always prayed the Breviary at around 4:00 in the afternoon, while at 5:00 he takes a walk either in the Vatican gardens or the garden of Castel Gandolfo, during which he prays the Rosary together with his secretary, Monsignor Georg Gänswein. In the winter, on the other hand, when it gets dark early, this walk takes place at 4:00. Toward 6:00, the regularly scheduled audiences are held. In the morning, there are the private audiences, in which he receives most importantly the bishops who come from abroad and heads of state, and so on, while the afternoon is reserved for the regularly scheduled audiences in which the heads of the various Curia offices give their reports and offer suggestions in matters in which the Pope must make a decision.

The evening meal is at 7:30; at 8:00 he watches the news. At around 8:30, he takes another short walk on the roof or, in the winter, in the corridors of the house. Afterward, Compline, the night prayer of the Church, is prayed, and with that his work day actually ends. Usually we sit down in the living room and talk for a while.

Do you also watch television together? Does the Holy Father have a favorite program?

Well, before the news, there used to be a television series *Inspector Rex*. We always used to watch it, because we like dogs, too. We are well acquainted with Herr Helmut Brossmann, the owner of the German shepherd "Rex" who plays the title role. He lives in the vicinity of Regensburg; he is also the manager of the Kastelruther Spatzen or the Augsburg Puppenkiste. He has even organized a few events for the Domspatzen. He is originally from the Sudetenland and converted to the Catholic faith a few years ago. A canon from the "Old Chapel" instructed him, and I was his confirmation sponsor. He is a great animal lover, and besides breeding German shepherds, including both of the dogs who portrayed "Rex", he has a whole zoo; furthermore, he is co-owner of the famous kennel that breeds Saint Bernards at the Great Saint Bernard Pass in the Alps. Other than that, my brother rarely watches television, at most a video film once in awhile that is related in some way to the Vatican or to a forthcoming canonization or beatification.

It is said that he reads aloud to you from the Breviary since your vision is no longer very good, while you play music for him ...

That is right; he prays the Breviary aloud: after Mass in the morning, Vespers in the afternoon, and Compline in the evening, because I can no longer pray them alone. In the evening, before we go to sleep, he sometimes asks me to play a song for him. Then I play for him on the piano a hymn or a folk song, for instance, "Im schönsten Wiesengrund", or night songs like "Der Mond ist aufgegangen" or "Adieu zur guten Nacht", just very simple things. In Advent or the Christmas season, of course, I play Christmas carols instead, whatever suits the occasion.

Does he go to bed rather early?

Yes, actually after the evening meal he does not work anymore; that was always the case. He can concentrate phenomenally throughout the day and works very quickly and efficiently. But he is not at all someone who works at night.

What does it mean for you to be "the Pope's brother" now?

Ah, personally, little has changed; more externally than interiorly. It is true, of course, that I am suddenly interesting to many people for whom I was previously nobody important. So I get many phone calls, from the press and other media, too; people often visit me, and I have been able to establish contacts that I did not have before. At first this led to a certain unrest in my life, but fortunately that has gradually ebbed away.

Otherwise, I must admit, not much has actually changed in my relationship with my brother, either. Only in prayer, then you present entirely different concerns to the dear Lord now. But still, the personal relationship has remained the same.

In Place of an Afterword:
Sixty Years a Priest (2011)

O n June 29, 2011, the Pope and his brother celebrated their "diamond priestly jubilee", the sixtieth anniversary of their ordination as priests on June 29, 1951, in the cathedral in Freising. Two days
previously, Monsignor Georg Ratzinger had flown to Rome for the occasion. After celebrating a private Mass in the private chapel of Benedict XVI,
he attended at 9:30 the great Pontifical Solemn High Mass for the Feast
of Saints Peter and Paul in Saint Peter's Basilica. Even though the almost
three-hour ceremony was centered on the bestowal of the pallium on forty
metropolitan bishops from twenty-four countries on four continents, Benedict XVI still recalled in his homily the day that left a more lasting impression on him than any other event in his truly eventful life: " 'I no longer
call you servants, but friends' (Jn 15:15). Sixty years on from the day of
my priestly ordination, I hear once again deep within me these words of
Jesus that were addressed to us new priests at the end of the ordination
ceremony by the Archbishop, Cardinal Faulhaber, in his slightly frail yet
firm voice. According to the liturgical practice of that time, these words conferred on the newly ordained priests the authority to forgive sins. . . . At
that moment I knew deep down that these words were no mere formality,
nor were they simply a quotation from Scripture. I knew that, at that
moment, the Lord himself was speaking to me in a very personal way. In
baptism and confirmation he had already drawn us close to him, he had
already received us into God's family. But what was taking place now was
something greater still. He calls me his friend. He welcomes me into the
circle of those he had spoken to in the Upper Room, into the circle of those
whom he knows in a very special way, and who thereby come to know him
in a very special way."

Shortly before his departure for Rome, I asked Georg Ratzinger for a résumé, so to speak, a look back on his own priesthood and the unusual career of his brother. Central to that interview, however, was the question of what it means in the first place to be a priest in our time.

Herr Domkapellmeister, when you look back on all these sixty years, in all honesty: Was your decision to enter the priesthood the right one; is it worthwhile to follow the Lord's call?

Absolutely! I cannot imagine at all how my life could have taken a different course. From childhood on, practically speaking, it was my goal, of which I never lost sight. And that is true of my brother, also: even though one thing or another did not develop as we had planned, nevertheless, the direction was clear from the beginning. So we both followed this path with all its consequences, and so today I can only say: I am heartily grateful to the dear Lord that he gave me the strength to travel this path without any ifs, ands, or buts. You simply sense his guidance and providence. Life holds certain difficulties in store for every human being, but if you have such a beautiful, fulfilling goal, if you sense that the Lord is near and you can follow so unwaveringly the way leading to him, then you can only exclaim with your whole heart: Deo gratias! (Thanks be to God!)

Does a priest receive more than he gives?

I think so; yes, you can put it that way!

When I gave a seminar in the Emmanuel School of Mission (ESM) in Altötting, I read the extraordinary motto of these young Christians who are involved in the missions, and I liked it very much: "Give all—get more!" Is that true also for priestly ministry?

Yes, by all means, that is correct. Above all, when a priest is engaged in pastoral care, when he then really makes an effort for the people and is not just watching the clock, he often receives infinitely rich blessings.

Unfortunately in B. for a time there was a pastor who publicly declared: "I don't let it burn me out!" That was a caricature of a priest, because anyone who thinks that way really should never have been allowed to be ordained. If someone really takes the care of souls to heart and sees in every human being he meets someone who wants to go to Christ, even though he knows that in the immediate situation the Lord's authority is expressed only in a weak priest, then he experiences such a great response, even from quarters where he actually would never have expected it. And I mean not just the gratitude of those with whom he deals directly; it comes then from quite different directions, also. That is when you first sense that it is really a blessing to be a priest. Someone who becomes a blessing for others is rewarded a thousandfold by the Lord and is then truly blessed. In that respect, the privilege of being a priest and serving the Lord is really a certain ideal.

What were the most beautiful moments in your priestly life?

That is difficult to say, actually. I have always understood my activity in the field of music to be pastoral work, also, for with everything we sang, even if it was not liturgical music, we tried to convey to people something of God's greatness. Even the secular pieces that do not lead us away from God communicate to us something of the glory of his creation.

But if you ask me about the most beautiful moments of my priestly life, then I have to say: It was always a solemn liturgy that we were able to help organize by means of magnificent music, in a beautiful church setting, in the worshipping community, when the people are reverent and a silence prevails that is not artificially created or commandeered but comes about on its own, precisely out of that reverence. A liturgy, though, in which the human senses are filled, too: the eye, the ear, and then the sense of smell through the incense, which also makes an important contribution. Those are indeed moments of happiness that you do not get in that form and intensity at a secular concert, however beautifully it is performed! This exaltation, this sense of being fulfilled and borne up at a Solemn High Mass come from somewhere else, after all, of that I am convinced!

Do you think that music is a subtler form of prayer?

I certainly could say that, yes! After all, the prayer of a human being, whether vocal prayer, common prayer, or even silent, private prayer, has its limits somewhere. Praise of God that is sung and set to music, in contrast, grips him holistically, not merely personally, the way he is. It lends him another, entirely new dimension, which vocal, mental, or meditative prayer cannot attain to the same extent.

Is music therefore also a path to God?

By all means, yes. It can also be a path leading away from him; think, for example, of the marching songs of the Hitler era or also the products of the secular entertainment industry, which only stir up human passions. Music can also be an instrument of the devil, but it is also an instrument of God.

Back to your brother, the Pope. In this conversation, we have reviewed his probably unique path from being a policeman's son to the leader of the universal Church, and it is time for the bottom line. What do you think? Does an unbroken thread run through the life of Benedict XVI, or was it an enormous accident that he finally became pope?

If you look at it from a purely human perspective, then of course it was chance. But when a believing person looks at his whole life, the way it unfolded, then he recognizes that it was a higher act of providence that led him purposefully to its goal— not to his! If you look at this path, how directly it actually ran: from a little acolyte to a theology student, then to an assistant pastor, an instructor, professor, prelate, bishop ... it is a stepladder in which each step had a particular meaning, on which he, practically speaking, kept moving forward, kept climbing a bit higher—not because he wanted it that way, not because he always advanced out of ambition, but because someone impelled him to take each of these steps, and he actually yielded only out of the conscientious fulfillment of his duty, constantly striving to perform the mission that was assigned to him.

There are many ambitious priests, indeed, regular careerists in the Church. Was he ever ambitious?

Personally, he was never ambitious, he really was not! But he was always conscientious and bore every responsibility that was imposed on him to the best of his ability. In doing so, he always had his doubts; he asked himself again and again whether he was really accomplishing in the best possible way what was being demanded of him, whether he was really doing everything he could to live up to the trust that others placed in him.

Did he ever consider even faintly the possibility of being elected pope?

No, he quite certainly did not. When Hans Küng claims that he was always striving for a position in the ecclesiastical hierarchy, that is sheer nonsense. I know him too well for that. He was convinced he had the special talent for explaining theology well and the grace to live this faith and to think correctly about it and that he was, therefore, actually a good teacher.

And that is precisely what he wanted to be, no more and no less; he saw that as his destiny. He never thought about any external honors in doing so; to him they were, instead, always unwelcome.

So he wanted simply to serve; as his motto says, he wanted to be a "co-worker of the truth" and to carry out this service well?

Quite right; that is exactly it.

And all the rest then happened automatically?

Yes, it happened by itself. I also know several priests who do their utmost to receive titles and honors, but that was never his style. He was always concerned about the matter at hand. He would like to perform his duty as well as he possibly can. For that reason, he has received certain talents along the way, and someday he will have to give an accounting of them.

In his first greeting to the people after his election as pope, he already called himself a "simple and humble laborer in the vineyard of the Lord" and that is probably quite honest, as he sees it. On meeting him, one notices that he is a profoundly humble, modest man. One always gets the impression that he approaches a matter rather tentatively and carefully, that he looks around first at how people are reacting to him. The applause, the honors, the presents, the jubilant crowds—all that seems unpleasant to him at first . . .

. . . precisely because he senses quite clearly this boundary between the man and the office and knows his limits. Of course, he knows that all this applies, not to him personally, but rather to him as a representative of a higher authority, as pope. He certainly knows how to make that distinction. As pope, a man must accept all that with an open heart; as a person, it would not suit him.

What do you wish him for the future?

I wish with all my heart that my brother will be spared health problems as much as possible and that he can always carry out well and unhindered his ministry as the successor of Peter. And then I wish that someday "on the other side", where we will all have to pass the exam (*Ex-Amen*), the final test, he will stand before the heavenly examiner and everything will end well; I am convinced, though, that it will.

After all, throughout his life, he has always asked first what God's will is and then wholeheartedly strove to follow him wherever he led him.

Acknowledgments

I thank all those who made it possible for this important testimony about the life of Pope Benedict XVI to be made public now.

In the first place, my heartfelt thanks go to Monsignor Georg Ratzinger. In the nine months between our first meeting and the publication of [the original German edition of] this book, I have repeatedly come to appreciate his modesty, amiability, and kindheartedness. I felt that each one of our meetings was a gift. I wholeheartedly thank also Monsignor Georg Gänswein, the personal secretary of His Holiness the Pope, for reviewing my manuscript quickly and for his valuable suggestions.

Without Roswitha Biersack from Deutschland pro Papa and her cooperative assistance, this project would never have materialized. She attended all our interviews, which she then transcribed, and accompanied the subsequent work on the manuscript. For this, a very cordial "Vergelt's Gott!" (May God reward you!) Of course my thanks go also to Frau Sabine Beschmann, who in one of the most difficult hours for the Catholic Church in Germany was godmother to the initiative Deutschland pro Papa, a mouthpiece and action league for all Catholics who are loyal to Rome.

Special thanks to His Excellency Bishop Gerhard Ludwig Müller, the Bishop of Regensburg, who was our host, as it were, but also to the organizers of the festive program to celebrate the diamond priestly jubilee of the Holy Father in Freising on June 18, 2011, especially Professor Doctor Rudolf Voderholzer from the Institute of Pope Benedict XVI. Thanks also, however, to Her Highness, Princess Gloria von Thurn und Taxis, for the lively intermezzo on the first day of our interviews. Then I thank my friends and supporters in Rome, among them Father Louis Thevalakara, [papal photographers] Arturo Mari and Francesco Sforza, and the co-workers of the Servizio Fotografico O.R. [*Osservatore Romano*], my colleagues [German and Austrian journalists] Paul Badde, Guido Horst, Michaela Koller, Benjamin Greschner, Peter Seewald, and Roland Noé.

In compiling the graphics, I was assisted by the Very Reverend Rupert Berger from Traunstein, who was in the same ordination class as Joseph and Georg Ratzinger, the archivist of the city of Traunstein, Franz Haselbeck, and Guido Treffler from the Archdiocesan Archives in Munich; the local historian and papal biographer Johann Nußbaum from Rimsting; the cheerful assistants at the Pope's house in Marktl am Inn, and Frau Kathi Stimmer-Salzeder, a local historian and church musician from Aschau. In addition, I thank Irmgard and Peter Huber, the residents of the Pope's house in Aschau, for their hospitality and helpfulness, Frau Kalweit of Regensburg for her valuable tips, and the "papal painter" Walter Andreas Angerer, Jr., for an inspiring meeting in Traunstein.

An especially cordial "Danke schön" goes to Frau Agnes Heindl, the housekeeper of the Cathedral Choirmaster, for her hospitality and refreshing cordiality—also on behalf of my dear dog Lucy, who could be separated from her kitchen only with difficulty.

My personal thanks to my fiancée Yuliya, who had to do without me during the weeks I spent in Bavaria, for her understanding and her constant inspiration. And, of course, I cannot forget my mother, Renate Hesemann, my media-savvy aunt, Angelika Puls, my aunt Ursula Niedermeier, her daughter, Christa Becker, and very creative grandson, Christian Becker.

Last but certainly not least, I thank my publisher, Frau Brigitte Fleissner-Mikorey, for her spontaneous enthusiasm, her commitment to and confidence in this project and the special circumstances in which it was carried out, my copyeditor, Doctor Iris Forster, Frau Anja Volkmer for the excellent public relations, and the whole publishing team at Herbig Verlag.

To all those also who cannot be named here but in one way or another contributed toward the development of this book, a sincere "Vergelt's Gott."

May it help others, also, to discover God's plan for their lives!

Abbreviations

The following abbreviations were used to identify the sources of quotations given in the text. More complete bibliographic information for some entries will be found in the bibliography that follows.

30 D   An interview with Alfred Läpple conducted by Gianni Valente and Pierluca Azzardo, *30 Days* 1 (1960), 60.

Heim   Maximilian Heinrich Heim, *Joseph Ratzinger: Life in the Church and Living Theology*, trans. Michael J. Miller (San Francisco: Ignatius Press, 2007).

IP   Seewald. *Benedict XVI: An Intimate Portrait.*

L   An interview with Cardinal Joseph Ratzinger by Martin Lohman on December 28, 1998, from *alpha forum br-online.de.*

LW   Benedict XVI, *Light of the World.*

M   Ratzinger, *Milestones.*

PF   Joseph Cardinal Ratzinger, *Pilgrim Fellowship of Faith: The Church as Communion*, trans. Henry Taylor (San Francisco: Ignatius Press, 2005).

SE   Ratzinger and Seewald, *Salt of the Earth.*

ST   Seewald, *Benedict XVI, Servant of the Truth.*

Bibliography

Asenkerschbaumer, Dionys, Winfried Helm, and Ludwig Raischl. *Geburtshaus Papst Benedikt XVI. Marktl am Inn.* Marktl, 2009.

Benedict XVI and Peter Seewald. *Light of the World.* Translated by Michael J. Miller and Adrian J. Walker. San Francisco: Ignatius Press, 2010.

Birkenseer, Karl. *Papst Benedikt XVI. in Regensburg.* Regensburg, 2006.

Borghese, Alessandra. *In the Footsteps of Joseph Ratzinger.* London, 2008.

Hamberger, Joachim. *Papst Benedikt XVI. in Freising.* Freising, 2007.

Hesemann, Michael. *Hitlers Religion.* Munich, 2004.

———. *Der Papst, der Hitler trotzte.* Augsburg, 2008.

——— and Yuliya Tkachova. *Benedetto! Benedikt XVI.—Die Kirche ist jung.* Munich, 2005.

Just, Barbara, and Jörg Hammann. *Mein Herz schlägt bayrisch.* Munich, 2006.

Kirchinger, Johann, and Ernst Schütz, eds. *Georg Ratzinger (1844–1899): Ein Leben zwischen Politik, Geschichte und Seelsorge.* Regensburg, 2008.

Kopp, Matthias, Arturo Mari, and Ludwig Ring-Eifel. *Der Papst in Bayern.* Freiburg, 2006.

Läpple, Alfred. *Benedikt XVI. und seine Wurzeln.* Augsburg, 2006.

Laube, Volker. *Das Erzbischöfliche Studienseminar Saint Michael in Traunstein und sein Archiv.* Regensburg, 2006.

Mai, Klaus. *Benedikt XVI.* Bergisch Gladbach, 2005.

Nußbaum, Johann. *"Ich werde mal Kardinal": Wurzeln, Kindheit und Jugend von Papst Benedikt XVI.* Rimsting, 2010.

———. *"Poetisch und herzensgut": Die Spuren des Papstes und seiner Familie in Rimsting.* Rimsting, 2006.

Pfister, Peter, ed. *Geliebte Heimat: Papst Benedikt XVI. und das Erzbistum München und Freising.* Munich, 2011.

———. *Joseph Ratzinger und das Erzbistum München und Freising.* Regensburg, 2006.

Ratzinger, Joseph. *God and the World.* Translated by Henry Taylor. San Francisco: Ignatius Press, 2002.

———. *Introduction to Christianity.* Translated by J. R. Foster and Michael J. Miller. San Francisco: Ignatius Press, 2004.

———. *Milestones: Memoirs: 1927–1977.* Translated by Erasmo Leiva-Merikakis. San Francisco: Ignatius Press, 1998.

———, and Peter Seewald. *Salt of the Earth.* Translated by Adrian Walker. San Francisco: Ignatius Press, 1997.

Salzeder, Kathi. *Joseph Ratzinger—Papst Benedikt XVI.: Kinderjahre in Aschau am Inn (1932–1937).* Aschau, 2006.

Seewald, Peter. *Benedict XVI: An Intimate Portrait.* Translated by Henry Taylor and Anne Englund Nash. San Francisco: Ignatius Press, 2008.

———, ed. *Benedict XVI, Servant of the Truth.* Translated by Brian McNeil. San Francisco: Ignatius Press, 2006.

Voderholzer, Rudolf, Christian Schaller, and Franz-Xaver Heibl, eds. *Mitteilungen Institut Benedikt XVI.* Volumes 1–3. Regensburg, 2008–2010.

Zuber, Anton *Der Bruder des Papstes: Georg Ratzinger und die Regensburger Domspatzen.* Freiburg, 2007.

Picture Credits

Collection of Johann Nußbaum, Rimsting: 21, 30
Anton Messerer, Rickering: 23
Collection of Michael Hesemann, Düsseldorf: 36, 42, 62
Wilma Jetzfellner, Chieming: 57
Irene Walter, Munich: 67, 87
Archives of the Pope's house in Marktl: 68
Archiv Kathi Stimmer-Salzeder, Gemeinde Aschau: 72, 85, 86
Josef Strehhuber, Steinhöring: 97
Archives of the city of Traunstein: 104, 148, 168
Peter Freiwang, Rosenheim: 121
Collection of Georg Ratzinger: 128, 129, 196
Archives of the Archdiocese of Munich: 161, 164, 212
Photo album of the First Mass of Doctor Rupert Berger in the archives of the city of Traunstein: 163 (Oswald Kettenberger, Traunstein), 167 (Gustl Tögl, Munich)
KNA-Bild, Bonn: 190
Ullstein Bild—Breuel-Bild, Berlin: 234
Photographic service of *L'Osservatore Romano*, Vatican City: 237, 240

Color plates:
Fotografia Felici, Rome, www.fotografiafelici.com: 1
Photographic service of *L'Osservatore Romano*, Vatican City: 2, 6–17
Collection of Georg Ratzinger: 3–5

Index of Names

(Page numbers of illustrations are italicized.)